HENRY WRIOTHESLEY, 3RD EARL OF SOUTHAMPTON

A MEMBER OF GRAY'S INN
SHAKESPEARE'S PATRON

SHAKESPEARE AND THE LAW

By
Sir DUNBAR PLUNKET BARTON, Bart.

WITH A FOREWORD BY
JAMES M. BECK

THE LAWBOOK EXCHANGE, LTD.
Clark, New Jersey

ISBN 9781584770008 (hardcover)
ISBN 9781616191313 (paperback)

Lawbook Exchange edition 2011

The quality of this reprint is equivalent to the quality of the original work.

THE LAWBOOK EXCHANGE, LTD.
33 Terminal Avenue
Clark, New Jersey 07066-1321

*Please see our website for a selection of our other publications
and fine facsimile reprints of classic works of legal history:*
www.lawbookexchange.com

Library of Congress Cataloging-in-Publication Data

Barton, D. Plunket (Dunbar Plunket), Sir, 1853-1937.
Shakespeare and the law / by Sir Dunbar Plunket Barton, bart.
with a foreword by James M. Beck.
p. cm.
Originally published: Boston : Houghton Mifflin Company, 1929.
ISBN 1-58477-000-7 (cloth : alk. paper)
1. Shakespeare, William, 1564-1616—Knowledge—Law. 2. Law
—Great Britain—History—16th century. 3. Law—Great Britain
—History—17th century. 4. Lawyers in literature. 5. Law in
literature. I. Title.
PR3028.B3 1999
822.3'3—dc21   99-26602
CIP

Printed in the United States of America on acid-free paper

SHAKESPEARE AND THE LAW

By
Sir DUNBAR PLUNKET BARTON, Bart.

WITH A FOREWORD BY
JAMES M. BECK

BOSTON AND NEW YORK
HOUGHTON MIFFLIN COMPANY
1929

THIS BOOK IS DEDICATED
TO
SIR ISRAEL GOLLANCZ
PROFESSOR OF ENGLISH LANGUAGE AND LITERATURE
IN THE UNIVERSITY OF LONDON
AND
CHAIRMAN OF THE SHAKESPEARE ASSOCIATION

CONTENTS

	LIST OF ILLUSTRATIONS	*page* ix
	FOREWORD BY THE HONOURABLE JAMES MONTGOMERY BECK	xiii
	INTRODUCTION	3
CH. I	LEGAL ALLUSIVENESS IN ELIZABETHAN DRAMA AND POETRY	7
II	THE INNS OF COURT—THE TEMPLE	17
III	THE INNS OF COURT—GRAY'S INN, AND LINCOLN'S INN	25
IV	THE INNS OF CHANCERY—CLEMENT'S INN	37
V	ALLUSIONS TO CASES AND LAWYERS OF NOTE—SIR WILLIAM GASCOIGNE, JUDGE HALES, AND JUDGE PHESANT	47
VI	ALLUSIONS TO CASES AND LAWYERS OF NOTE—SIR EDWARD COKE, SIR TOBY AND SIR HOBY, AND CHIEF BARON MANWOOD	59

CONTENTS

VII ALLUSIONS TO CASES AND LAWYERS OF NOTE—SHELLEY'S CASE, FINES AND RECOVERIES, AND THE CASE OF PERPETUITIES *page* 69

VIII ALLUSIONS TO COURTS AND PROCEDURE 81

IX ALLUSIONS TO CROWN, CRIMINAL, CONSTITUTIONAL AND FEUDAL LAW 91

X ALLUSIONS TO CROWN, CRIMINAL, CONSTITUTIONAL AND FEUDAL LAW (continued) 101

XI ALLUSIONS TO THE LAW OF REAL PROPERTY 111

XII SHAKESPEARE'S USE OF LEGAL MAXIMS 121

XIII SHAKESPEARE'S USE OF LEGAL JARGON 131

XIV LORD CAMPBELL'S EXAGGERATION OF SHAKESPEARE'S LEGAL ACQUIREMENTS 141

XV OTHER EXAGGERATIONS OF SHAKESPEARE'S LEGAL ACQUIREMENTS 153

INDEX 161

ILLUSTRATIONS

HENRY WRIOTHESLEY, THIRD EARL OF SOUTHAMPTON: A MEMBER OF GRAY'S INN: SHAKESPEARE'S PATRON *Frontispiece*

WILLIAM CECIL, BARON OF BURGHLEY: A MEMBER OF GRAY'S INN: MASTER OF THE COURT OF WARDS   26

HENRY CAREY, FIRST LORD HUNSDON: A MEMBER OF GRAY'S INN: LORD CHAMBERLAIN TO QUEEN ELIZABETH   28

SIR PHILIP SIDNEY: A MEMBER OF GRAY'S INN   30

WILLIAM HERBERT, THIRD EARL OF PEMBROKE: A MEMBER OF GRAY'S INN: LORD CHAMBERLAIN TO KING JAMES I   32

SIR WALTER RALEIGH: A MEMBER OF THE MIDDLE TEMPLE   60

SIR ROGER MANWOOD: A MEMBER OF THE INNER TEMPLE: LORD CHIEF BARON OF THE EXCHEQUER UNDER QUEEN ELIZABETH   66

SIR EDWARD COKE: A MEMBER OF THE INNER TEMPLE: LORD CHIEF JUSTICE OF THE KING'S BENCH UNDER KING JAMES I   76

ILLUSTRATIONS

SIR WILLIAM GASCOIGNE: A MEMBER OF GRAY'S INN: LORD CHIEF JUSTICE OF THE KING'S BENCH UNDER KING HENRY IV   82

THE COURT OF KING'S BENCH IN THE TIME OF THE PLANTAGENETS   92

HENRY WRIOTHESLEY, THIRD EARL OF SOUTHAMPTON: A MEMBER OF GRAY'S INN: SHAKESPEARE'S PATRON   106

THE COURT OF WARDS, PRESIDED OVER BY LORD BURGHLEY   144

FOREWORD

SHAKESPEARE is one of the most interesting, yet baffling, enigmas of History. While his 'gentle' personality is clearly revealed by his writings, yet his myriad-minded soul has mysterious recesses which we can never fathom. Like his own Hamlet, he sardonically smiles at the futile attempt of later generations to sound the greatest depths of his nature and to each he says, like Hamlet,

Why, look you now, how unworthy a thing you make of me! You would play upon me; you would seem to know my stops; you would pluck out the heart of my mystery; you would sound me from my lowest note to the top of my compass: and there is much music, excellent voice, in this little organ; yet cannot you make it speak. 'Sblood, do you think I am easier to be played on than a pipe? Call me what instrument you will, though you can fret me, yet you cannot play upon me.

Among the many questions which have been suggested by our ignorance of the fuller details of his life, his connection with the laws and lawyers of his time is among the most interesting. He has been credited with a profound knowledge of the law, and especially of legal phraseology, which

FOREWORD

has not only given rise to the conjecture that he may have been in his earlier years a lawyer, or a lawyer's clerk, but to the more fanciful contention that his great contemporary, Francis Bacon, wrote the plays. This problem, like Banquo's ghost, will 'not down,' and it is this circumstance that gives an especial interest to this book.

It gives a more accurate idea than any, of which I know, that Shakespeare's knowledge of legal phraseology falls far short of proving that he was a lawyer at any period of his life. Even though he had studied law, of which there is no direct proof, there would still remain the gross improbability that Francis Bacon, in addition to his many public duties and literary labors, could possibly have added the plays of Shakespeare.

I imagine that both Sir Dunbar Plunket Barton and the writer of this introduction would have been glad, in one respect only, to have reached a different conclusion and one more favorable to the Baconian theory, for we are both Benchers of Gray's Inn, of which Bacon was not only the official head, but also the master spirit in those 'spacious days of Queen Elizabeth.' Here he lived and worked the greater part of his life, and to his chambers in Gray's Inn he came after his impeachment and disgrace, to pursue, in the years that remained to

FOREWORD

him, his philosophical studies. While he had other residences in London, he took the greatest delight in his associations with the Inn and it is probable that many of his acknowledged works were written there. If he were the author of the plays commonly attributed to Shakespeare, it is probable that he would have written many of them in Gray's Inn. To those who love the Inn, it would be a matter of immense pride to believe that this venerable nursery of legal learning, which still remains one of the most fascinating relics of Tudor days, was the place where 'Hamlet' was written, as well as the 'Advancement of Learning.'

I must confess, however, that even this added glory of the Inn, were it possible, would not wholly reconcile me to the idea that the man, who so shamelessly betrayed his friend and patron, Essex, was the man who wrote plays in which the vice of ingratitude was denounced above every other human failing. Moreover, I am loath to believe that the sublimity of Shakespeare's moral philosophy, its supreme faith in justice, should have been written by one, who so shamelessly betrayed the trust reposed in him, as Lord Chancellor Bacon did when he accepted bribes from litigants.

The true lover of Shakespeare naturally hesi-

FOREWORD

tates to dignify the Baconian theory with any discussion, for it has been well said by some great Shakespearean editor that there is only one man who is more unreasonable than the Baconian, and that is the man who attempts to argue the question with him. Of this I had, about twenty years ago, an amusing illustration, which it may be well to record in this introduction. It shows how a strong and vigorous mind, when infected with the virus of the Baconian theory, can lose all sense of proportion and follow a line and method of reasoning, which, if applied to any other problem, would be supremely ridiculous.

It was my privilege to know Mark Twain in his last years. My acquaintance with him originated in our common affection for the late Henry H. Rogers. In the year 1909, Mr. Rogers had completed a railroad which he had built with his own funds at an expense of over thirty millions of dollars. The Chamber of Commerce of Norfolk, Virginia, the terminus of the railroad, signalized its completion by giving a dinner to the great man of affairs, who, at a great hazard to his personal fortunes, had so munificently constructed the railroad from his own resources. Mr. Rogers invited Mark Twain and the writer of this introduction to be his personal guests at that dinner and, in the course of an address that I made, I quoted

FOREWORD

some passages from Shakespeare. This interested Mark Twain and, after Mr. Rogers's death, which took place a few months later, Mark Twain invited me to come to his home at Stormfield to discuss the authorship of Shakespeare's plays. He had previously sent me a book, which he had recently written on the subject and which bore the fanciful title, 'Is Shakespeare Dead?' Upon the flyleaf he had written the following:

There's mountains of history to prove that the human being will not take the real thing when he can get a fetish in place of it.

To Mark Twain, the 'fetish' was the opinion, accepted for over three centuries, that Shakespeare had written his plays.

The receipt of this book was followed by a letter, dated April 25, 1909, which concluded:

You must come up here and give me a week-end — then we'll discuss and discuss. Name a date, won't you, that will be to your convenience? and let me know.

While it was a privilege to spend a week-end with the great humorist and philosopher, whose end was even then fast approaching, yet I confess the prospect of discussing this stale problem with a fanatical Baconian was not alluring. I had read his book and had not been impressed with the

FOREWORD

soundness of its reasoning, although his chief argument, that the plays indubitably disclosed the fact that the dramatist must have been a lawyer, had always given me some concern. The book indicated that Mark Twain's doubts had not been of recent origin, but that he had considered the question for many years. Curiously enough, he tells us in the opening chapter that when he was an assistant pilot on a Mississippi steamer in his early years, he would often discuss the subject with the chief pilot, one Ealer. While guiding the boat in the tortuous channels of the Mississippi, Ealer would quote reams of Shakespeare's verse to his admiring friend and assistant. Frequently, the discussion turned upon the theory, then recently advanced by a Miss Delia Bacon (who a few years later ended her career in an insane asylum) that the true author of the plays was Francis Bacon.

Because of the curious sequel that followed in my own discussion with Mark Twain, I venture to quote from 'Is Shakespeare Dead?' Mark Twain, commenting on the manner in which Ealer argued the Baconian theory, writes:

He did his arguing with heat, with energy, with violence; and I did mine with the reserve and moderation of a subordinate who does not like to be flung out of a pilot-house that is perched forty feet above the

FOREWORD

water. He was fiercely loyal to Shakespeare and cordially scornful of Bacon and of all the pretensions of the Baconians.

Mark Twain proceeds to tell us that he soon became a believer in the Baconian theory, boldly accepted battle with his superior and confounded his opponent by the argument that, if Shakespeare had in his plays used a large number of technical terms, which were only known to pilots, the conclusion would follow irresistibly that the author must have been a pilot. Apparently Ealer could not answer this remarkable analogy and Mark Twain adds:

> It was a triumph for me. He was silent awhile and I knew what was happening: he was losing his temper. And I knew he would presently close the session with the same old argument that was always his stay and support in time of need; the same old argument, the one I couldn't answer, that I was an ass and better shut up. He delivered it and I obeyed.

When I reached Mark Twain's home and my baggage had been taken by the valet, Mark Twain took me into the library and went at his favorite topic as abruptly as Hamlet made the players 'give a taste of their quality.' We were 'e'en to't like French falconers, fly at anything we see.' As Mark Twain was then well advanced in years and had spent sufficient time in contro-

FOREWORD

versial strife to realize the absurdity of a loss of temper in any discussion, I should have supposed that he would have discussed the question temperately and soberly, but the event proved that he was as incapable of this moderation as was Ealer fifty years before on the Mississippi steamboat. As the discussion proceeded, I naturally suggested some of the many arguments, which, if documentary history has any value, support the claims of the Stratford poet. The more I submitted the arguments for his consideration, the more passionate his temper became. At first, I regarded this with some amusement, but later with some concern. Finally, when I advanced some argument to which he could not give even a plausible answer, he suddenly burst into a volley of profanity, worthy of his early days on the Mississippi, and cursed and reviled Shakespeare with a virulence of phrase that would have done justice to Falstaff and his companions. After this explosion, he sullenly went into the billiard room and commenced to knock the balls idly about, while I went up to my room and considered whether I should pack my valises and make my adieus. We met again at dinner, but nothing was said about the disputed question, nor in the few remaining days of my visit. On the following morning, we took a long walk over the hills of

FOREWORD

Connecticut and no one could have been more delightful than Mark Twain. We ran the whole gamut of human problems and always in good temper, and I gained a clearer idea of his original and, generally, noble mind than I had at any previous time, but neither of us ventured to refer again to the controversial subject.

Nothing better illustrates the pernicious effect upon the reasoning power of a vigorous mind than the fanatical interest which Mark Twain took in the Baconian theory. It became an obsession with him and, as with so many other vigorous minds who have been infected with the virus, he lost all sense of proportion in his reasoning. Had he been merely an academic scholar, this would not have been so strange, for, when the 'wish is father to the thought,' it is pitiful how far astray a scholarly mind can go. But Mark Twain was a man of the world and his wits had been sharpened in the keen competition of life. He was a realist and generally reasoned soundly. But, like most Baconians, he lost alike his humor and poise when his mind dwelt upon this subject. His Boswell, Albert Bigelow Paine, records the following conversation in 1908:

Mark Twain said, 'I *know* that Shakespeare did not write those plays and I have reason to believe he did not touch the text in any way.'

FOREWORD

'How can you be so positive?' I asked.

He replied: 'I have private knowledge from a source that cannot be questioned.'

When Paine expressed his surprise, he found that he was 'clearly in earnest,' and Mark Twain added, quite seriously,

It is the great discovery of the age. The world will soon ring with it. I wish I could tell you about it, but I have passed my word. You will not have long to wait.

Paine then sailed for the Mediterranean and awaited word from Mark Twain as to the great discovery, but no word came. On his return to Stormfield, he eagerly asked Mark Twain whether the mysterious discovery had yet been announced to the world and was told, again to quote his biographer, that

the matter had been delayed, but that he was no longer required to suppress it; that the revelation was in the form of a book — a book which revealed conclusively to any one, who would take the trouble to follow the directions, that the acrostic name of Francis Bacon in a great variety of forms ran through many — probably through all — of the so-called Shakespeare plays. He said it was far and away beyond anything of the kind ever published; that Ignatius Donnelly and others had merely glimpsed the truth, but that the author of this book, William Stone

FOREWORD

Booth, *had demonstrated, beyond any doubt or question, that the Bacon signatures were there.*

The Booth book soon appeared and Mark Twain and Paine spent many an evening in working out the great cipher in accordance with the Booth formula and Paine records that Mark Twain even

confessed that his faculties had been more or less defeated in attempting to follow the ciphers, and he complained bitterly that the evidence had not been set forth so that he who merely skims a book might grasp it.

However, they pursued their cabalistic studies and apparently Mark Twain's sense of humor had entirely deserted him. Paine records that it was 'an interesting, if not wholly convincing, occupation,' yet Mark Twain never doubted and was so completely convinced that Bacon wrote the plays and concealed his authorship — of which he had no occasion to be ashamed — by a cipher that on one occasion, when he had just witnessed a performance of 'Romeo and Juliet,' he said, 'That is about the best play that Lord Bacon ever wrote.'

It is certainly a reflection upon the reasoning powers of a concededly vigorous mind and certainly upon his sense of humor that Mark

FOREWORD

Twain could have seriously taken the claptrap of this, or any, pretended cipher, but to the Baconian nothing is incredible. He can read a connected cipher history through the plays, as printed in the First Folio, and can blandly ignore the fact that the plays were put together seven years after Shakespeare's death and with so little method or purpose that 'Troilus and Cressida' was at the last moment interpolated in the middle of the volume. The man who could suppose that these plays, written at different times in a period of over twenty years, and only published after the author's death, could contain a connected cipher, which on the theory of the hidden cipher was necessarily designed at the time the plays were written, is quite capable of believing that the moon is made of green cheese.

One argument I could have advanced on that occasion to Mark Twain, but refrained from doing so, because I have always appreciated the force of Dr. Johnson's maxim that discussion is at an end when personalities are introduced. I have in mind the fact that the principal argument, generally advanced to prove, *a priori*, that Shakespeare could not have written his plays, could be used with even greater force to prove that Mark Twain never wrote his books. The basic argument of the Baconian theory is that a country

FOREWORD

boy, who, it is assumed, had a very limited education and who came to London at an early age, could not, by any possibility, have written within the next twenty years thirty-six plays, of which twenty are acknowledged masterpieces, especially as the plays disclose a wide knowledge of human life.

The same argument could be applied with even greater force to Mark Twain. Here was a boy, who was born in a little Missouri village of fifty houses; had little school education and certainly none that was comparable with the very excellent guild school at Stratford, and whose early environment, although somewhat better than that of the parentless waif, Huckleberry Finn, differed little from that of Tom Sawyer, whom he so graphically drew from his own life and experience. The little border town was the last place that one would imagine as a nursery of genius. At nine he runs away from home, as a stowaway on one of the Mississippi boats, but is caught and sent home; at eighteen he becomes a tramp printer and for fifteen months wandered from city to city in search of work. Then he becomes a 'cub pilot' on one of the Mississippi steamboats and, notwithstanding Ealer's interest in Shakespeare, it is quite evident that about him were men of meagre education. Then he wanders across the

FOREWORD

great plains to the Far West and becomes a prospector in a mining camp and finally drifts into village journalism. Then he became a lecturer and finally drifts to New York, where he delighted the world with the unique travel sketches of 'Innocents Abroad.'

Shakespeare said that 'home-keeping youths have ever homely wits,' and it is quite evident that Mark Twain, who never had a college education, or even an elementary training, acquired all his knowledge in that greatest of all universities, the 'College of Hard Knocks.'

Notwithstanding this very unpromising beginning for an author, Mark Twain writes at least thirty volumes and, while the content is of very uneven merit, yet the best of his works seem destined, in an age of voluminous and ephemeral literature, to be permanent additions to the world's narrowing lists of classics. If his books had dealt only with life on the Mississippi, or in the Nevada mining camps, there would be no occasion for surprise that a keen mind could have taken such unusual scenes and made of them permanent additions to literature. But Mark Twain's collected works cover many matters, which he never could have learned on a Mississippi steamboat, or in a Nevada mining camp. They show a very considerable range of study

FOREWORD

and, while his style is as uneven in merit as the substance of the text, yet there are 'purple passages,' which are not unworthy of the great masters of English prose. He had the reasoning of a philosopher, the imagination of a poet, and a real gift for beautiful prose, which, taking him at his best, makes him a great writer.

Reasoning, *a priori*, there is nothing more incredible than that an uneducated wanderer from Missouri could have ascended the heights that Mark Twain reached. By comparison, the Shakespeare problem is comparatively easy, for Shakespeare had an excellent training in the grammar school at Stratford, certainly studied Latin and probably Greek, and, if we are to believe the only authentic record as to the missing years (1587–92), which we have from the old chronicler of the Restoration theatre, Beaston, he was during those missing five years a 'school teacher in the country.' As such, he could well have pursued the studies of the classics, which he began at Stratford. Whether this is so or not, the fact remains that Shakespeare's natural advantages, so far as we know them, were rich in comparison with those of Mark Twain and, if the *a priori* argument of incapacity from lack of education applies in Shakespeare's case, it applies with even greater strength in Mark Twain's case.

FOREWORD

I sometimes regret that I did not advance this argument to Mark Twain in our discussion, but his anger would probably have not been lessened by so personal an allusion, and yet it might have gone far to convince him that the wholly gratuitous assumption that a genius could not produce great work, unless he had a college education, is unwarranted. Franklin is another illustration. He had only the crudest elementary education for two years and yet became the greatest and most versatile intellectual genius of his age, and one of its most accomplished writers. His literary style has stood the test of time far better than that of either Addison or Doctor Johnson, and yet he had no education after his twelfth year, except in the Great University of Life.

The only other argument for the Baconian theory, which has ever given any rational human being reason for pause, is that the writer of the plays must have been a lawyer and that there is no reason to believe that Shakespeare was a lawyer. Even if this were so, why Bacon? He was not the sole lawyer of those spacious days. This is Mark Twain's main argument in his 'Is Shakespeare Dead?' He says:

If I were required to superintend a Bacon-Shakespeare controversy, I would narrow the matter to a single question — the only one, so far as the previous

FOREWORD

controversies have informed me, concerning which illustrious experts of unimpeachable competency have testified: '*Was the author of Shakespeare's Works a lawyer?*' — a lawyer deeply read and of limitless experience? I would put aside the guesses, and surmises, and perhapses, and might-have-beens, and could-have-beens, and must-have-beens, and we-are-justified-in-presumings, and the rest of those vague spectres and shadows and indefinitenesses, and stand or fall, win or lose, by the verdict rendered by the jury upon that single question. If the verdict was Yes, I should feel quite convinced that the Stratford Shakespeare, the actor, manager, and trader who died so obscure, so forgotten, so destitute of even village consequence that sixty years afterward no fellow-citizen and friend of his later days remembered to tell anything about him, did not write the Works.

The argument was an old one. It was first advanced by Malone, who seems to have been a more acute Shakespeare commentator than a lawyer, although the law was his profession. The argument had its greatest vogue when Lord Chief Justice Campbell, in 1859, published a book called, 'Shakespeare's Legal Requirements.' The Lord Chief Justice, with an unusual disregard of the value of testimony, delivered the sententious judgment that only a lawyer could possibly have written the plays. He found that Shakespeare had 'a deep technical knowledge of the law,' and an easy familiarity with 'some of

FOREWORD

the most abstruse proceedings in English jurisprudence.' Later the Lord Chief Justice says, 'Whenever he indulges this propensity, he uniformly lays down good law.'

Most lawyers know that Lord Campbell was more famed for his brilliancy than for his accuracy, but, outside of the profession, it is not unnatural that the solemn judgment of a Lord Chief Justice, who subsequently became Lord Chancellor, should have made a profound impression upon many men. Even the editors, who would not renounce the orthodox view as to the authorship, felt obliged to follow Lord Chief Justice Campbell in praising the accuracy of Shakespeare's use of legal phraseology, and the Lord Chancellor was followed by other eminent jurists, notably, Lord Penzance, who speaks of Shakespeare's

profound familiarity with not only the principles, axioms and maxims, but the technicalities of English law, a knowledge so perfect and intimate that he was never incorrect and never at fault.

All this argument was summed up in Greenwood's 'The Shakespeare Problem Restated,' which had appeared in 1908 and which powerfully influenced Mark Twain to contribute his argument to the problem.

The value of Sir Plunket Barton's book lies in

FOREWORD

the fact that he saps the foundation of this argument. He shows that a use of legal phraseology was a common characteristic of the dramatists of Elizabeth's time and that many of Shakespeare's rivals, who were not lawyers, were more addicted to such phraseology than Shakespeare. He also shows that Shakespeare was often inaccurate in his legal phraseology and that, at best, his allusions were of that superficial character, which in a litigious age would characterize the common speech of the fervent spirits of that brilliant era.

I must apologize to the reader and to the author of the book for this long discourse on the Shakespeare-Bacon theory. I have only referred to it to emphasize the illuminating character of Sir Plunket Barton's contribution to the subject, but I cannot forbear from giving one argument of my own on the subject, which has always seemed to me to have some value.

'The style is the man,' said Buffon, and every writer has his individual style. It is not difficult to distinguish between such styles. Let me contrast two excerpts from Shakespeare and Bacon which, to some extent, deal with a common theme, the theatre. The first is from Bacon's 'Essays' and is a short treatise on the method whereby a masque (a form of dramatic entertainment) should be given, and the other is

FOREWORD

Hamlet's advice to the players. If my reader will now read both in succession and shall then be of the opinion that the same literary craftsman wrote both, he will greatly surprise me. The conclusion seems reasonable that different men wrote the two excerpts. The one is the work of a solemn pedant, and the other that of an actor and poet; the one had no literary style and the other had a style whose crystalline beauty is like that of a mountain brook.

Bacon thus writes of 'Masques and Triumphs':

These things are but toys, to come amongst such serious observations. But yet, since princes will have such things, it is better they should be graced with elegancy, than daubed with cost. Dancing to song is a thing of great state and pleasure. I understand it, that the song be in quire, placed aloft, and accompanied with some broken music; and the ditty fitted to the device. Acting in song, especially in dialogues, hath an extreme good grace: I say acting, not dancing (for that is a mean and vulgar thing); and the voices of the dialogue would be strong and manly (a bass and a tenor, no treble); and the ditty high and tragical, not nice or dainty. Several quires, placed one over against another, and taking the voice by catches, anthem-wise, give great pleasure. Turning dances into figure is a childish curiosity. And generally, let it be noted, that those things which I here set down are such as do naturally take the sense, and not respect petty wonderments. It is true, the alterations of

FOREWORD

scenes, so it be quietly and without noise, are things of great beauty and pleasure; for they feed and relieve the eye, before it be full of the same object. Let the scenes abound with light, specially coloured and varied; and let the masquers, or any other, that are to come down from the scene, have some motions upon the scene itself before their coming down; for it draws the eye strangely, and makes it with great pleasure to desire to see that it cannot perfectly discern. Let the songs be loud and cheerful, and not chirpings or pulings. Let the music likewise be sharp and loud and well placed. The colours that shew best by candle-light are white, carnation, and a kind of sea-water-green; and oes, or spangs, as they are of no great cost, so they are of most glory. As for rich embroidery, it is lost and not discerned. Let the suits of the masquers be graceful, and such as become the person when the vizars are off: not after examples of known attires; Turks, soldiers, mariners, and the like. Let antimasques not be long; they have been commonly of fools, satyrs, baboons, wild-men, antics, beasts, sprites, witches, Ethiopes, pigmies, turquets, nymphs, rustics, Cupids, statuas moving, and the like. As for angels, it is not comical enough to put them in antimasques; and anything that is hideous, as devils, giants, is on the other side as unfit. But chiefly, let the music of them be recreative, and with some strange changes. Some sweet odours, suddenly coming forth, without any drops falling, are, in such a company as there is steam and heat, things of great pleasure and refreshment. Double masques, one of men, another of ladies, addeth state and variety.

FOREWORD

But all is nothing, except the room be kept clear and neat.

And now compare the passage in which Hamlet gives the following advice to the players:

Speak the speech, I pray you, as I pronounced it to you, trippingly on the tongue; but if you mouth it, as many of your players do, I had as lief the town-crier spoke my lines. Nor do not saw the air too much with your hand, thus, but use all gently; for in the very torrent, tempest, and, as I may say, the whirlwind of passion, you must acquire and beget a temperance that may give it smoothness. O, it offends me to the soul to hear a robustious periwig-pated fellow tear a passion to tatters, to very rags, to split the ears of the groundlings, who for the most part are capable of nothing but inexplicable dumb-shows and noise. I would have such a fellow whipped for o'erdoing Termagant; it out-herods Herod; pray you, avoid it.

Be not too tame neither, but let your own discretion be your tutor: suit the action to the word, the word to the action; with this special observance, that you o'erstep not the modesty of nature: for any thing so overdone is from the purpose of playing, whose end, both at the first and now, was and is, to hold, as 'twere, the mirror up to nature; to show virtue her own feature, scorn her own image, and the very age and body of the time his form and pressure. Now this overdone, or come tardy off, though it make the unskilful laugh, cannot but make the judicious grieve; the censure of the which one must in your allowance o'erweigh a whole theatre of others. O, there be play-

FOREWORD

ers that I have seen play, and heard others praise, and that highly, not to speak it profanely, that, neither having the accent of Christians, nor the gait of Christian, pagan, nor man, have so strutted and bellowed that I have thought some of nature's journeymen had made men and not made them well, they imitated humanity so abominably.

I selected these two excerpts because both were in prose and both related to some extent to the same subject. Obviously, it would be quite unfair to contrast a prose selection from Bacon's 'Essays' with a poetical effusion of Shakespeare in blank verse or lyric form. Bacon's essay suggests the learned justice, 'full of wise saws and modern instances.' Nowhere is there the suggestion of either imagination or feeling. He writes pedantically and dogmatically. Never once does he illuminate his meaning with a metaphor or analogy. He lays down the law of 'Masques and Triumphs' as if he were reading a decision from the Bench. He is giving his readers the benefit of his experience in phrases that are colorless.

When, however, we turn to the Shakespeare excerpt, we perceive at once the man of imagination and feeling. No one was more addicted to the use of metaphor and analogy than Shakespeare, and this excerpt is, in this respect, no exception. The reader will be impressed with the

FOREWORD

passionate earnestness of the speech. One feels that the writer feels deeply on the subject which he discusses. It almost suggests a personal grievance, especially if I had given the full quotation, where Shakespeare rebukes the clowns for saying more than is set down for them. The reader feels that the writer of these lines took a passionate interest in the theatre and had a high conception of its ideals. He can feel the sensitiveness of the poet, who writes beautiful lines only to hear them mangled in oral delivery.

It cannot be seriously questioned that Shakespeare was an actor, a poet, and a dramatist, and these lines are those which one would naturally suppose a dramatic poet of high ideals would write in connection with the production of his plays.

The essential point, however, is the difference in literary style and intellectual method. If Bacon wrote both excerpts, we would look for some similarity between them, and for this we look in vain.

Assuming that Shakespeare's knowledge of legal phraseology was more than the ordinary, unless he had legal training, the argument that he could not have written the plays because he had no legal training ignores the fact that we do not know exactly what Shakespeare did after he left

FOREWORD

Stratford. Apart from some unreliable traditions, there is only Beaston's testimony, to which reference has already been made, that Shakespeare, after he left Stratford, was for some years a school teacher. For all that appears, he may have been for a time a student in one of the Inns of Court. Young men of good families — and Shakespeare was such — were often sent to the Inns of Court, even though they did not intend to become lawyers.

While there is no evidence that Shakespeare was a student in any one of the Inns, yet, if he had been a student in Gray's Inn, it would explain several facts, which, in the absence of any explanation, are somewhat puzzling. One of them is the asserted familiarity with legal phraseology, and the other, his intimacy with the Earl of Southampton and other nobles of Elizabeth's Court. Southampton, Pembroke, and Montgomery were all students of Gray's Inn, as were Bacon and Cecil. The friendly relations, which apparently existed between this Stratford boy and so great a noble as the Earl of Southampton, could thus be easily explained and in the atmosphere of the Inn, Shakespeare, although not studying for the Bar, would have heard much of the jargon of the law and pending litigation in the courts.

FOREWORD

However, I will not imitate Mark Twain by thus giving to 'airy nothings a local habitation and a name,' for I freely admit that there is no evidence, either documentary or of tradition, which gives any color to the conjecture. It is enough that Shakespeare, with an acquisitive genius, such as has rarely, if ever, been given to any man, — living in an age when the two great movements of the time, that of the Reformation and of the Renaissance, flowed in a common channel and reached their flood tide in London, — absorbed the learning of the time, even as Mark Twain, in his wanderings and travels, absorbed sufficient learning to write a scholarly history like that of 'Joan of Arc,' and to discuss with power and understanding many of the great problems of art, literature, and history. If it be said that the analogy between Shakespeare and Mark Twain fails because the writings of the one are so incomparably superior to the other, the answer inevitably is that the genius of Mark Twain, as compared with that of Shakespeare, is that of our Sun to Betelgeuse.

As the personality of the author is generally of interest to the reader, let me add that Sir Dunbar Plunket Barton, as a former Solicitor-General of Ireland, a Justice of the High Court of Ireland, Member of Parliament, and a member

FOREWORD

of many important boards and commissions, writes with authority on this or any subject pertaining to English jurisprudence. In addition, he has an intimate knowledge of the Elizabethan era, and especially of the Inns of Court, and has contributed several books to the history of the Inns.

Concluding this foreword, I am impressed with the fact that no foreword is necessary. If 'good wine needs no bush' and a 'good play no epilogue,' then a good book needs no foreword. The book speaks for itself and should appeal alike to students of law and literature.

JAMES M. BECK
Former Solicitor-General of the United States

WASHINGTON, D.C.
June 15, 1928

LINKS BETWEEN SHAKESPEARE AND THE LAW

BY

THE RIGHT HONOURABLE SIR DUNBAR PLUNKET BARTON

BART., K.C., D.LITT.

INTRODUCTION

THIS book originally appeared in serial form in the *Law Journal*. It collects the various links which are discoverable between Shakespeare and the Law, and distributes them under three principal heads. His relation to the Inns of Court and of Chancery are dealt with in Chapters II, III and IV. His references to great Judges, famous advocates and celebrated trials are discussed in Chapters V, VI, and VII.

The rest of the book is taken up with his legal allusions—a path which has been trodden by previous writers. This book adopts a new method of arrangement. The poet's legal allusions are classified from a lawyer's point of view under the various branches of the Law to which they respectively belong, and the most important ones are given in connexion with their context. This method of arrangement is intended to help the reader to estimate their range, and to observe Shakespeare's methods

INTRODUCTION

of transmuting legal ideas into poetry and into dramatic dialogue.

The subject of Shakespeare's legal allusions has usually been approached from a controversial angle. But this volume was not written with a controversial aim. The Author is a follower of the orthodox opinion that the Shakespearian plays and poems were written by William Shakespeare of Stratford-on-Avon; but he has not concerned himself with that vexed question, and he disclaims any intention of meddling with it.

The book contains, here and there (for example in Chapter VII), some new suggestions which the Author submits respectfully to the judgment of his legal brethren in Great Britain, in Ireland, and in the United States.

LEGAL ALLUSIVENESS IN ELIZABETHAN DRAMA AND POETRY

CHAPTER I

LEGAL ALLUSIVENESS IN ELIZABETHAN DRAMA AND POETRY

THE easy use which Shakespeare made of legal topics has caused some of his commentators to jump to the conclusion that, at some stage of his career, he had been a lawyer or a lawyer's clerk. This theory is not supported by any extrinsic evidence or by any tradition; and there does not appear to be any necessity for resorting to it. Most of Shakespeare's legalisms were drawn either from the history of the Plantagenet and Tudor periods, from the procedure of Courts of Justice, from the jargon of the Law of Real Property, or from certain notorious aspects of the Criminal and Constitutional Law of his time. These were subjects which had many avenues of approach to his mind.

SHAKESPEARE AND THE LAW

In the Elizabethan age, writes Mr. Hubert Hall, of the Public Record Office, in an oft-quoted passage, 'every man was up to a certain point his own lawyer', and 'was well versed in all the technical forms and procedure'. The public took a keener interest in legal proceedings than they do in our time. There were fewer places of recreation, and people with idle time on their hands were more disposed to haunt the Courts for the purpose of whiling it away. Drayton, in his *Polyolbion*, described a typical Court scene, where a crowd of listeners hung upon the lips of the Judge as he delivered a learned and reasoned judgment at the end of a great case.

There was much to impress the imagination of spectators in the ceremonial side of the administration of the Law, and in the solemnity and impartiality of judicial proceedings in non-political cases. There was an element of '*Grand Guignol*' in the ferocity of prosecutions for treason and in the spectacular barbarity of public executions. Legal procedure also had its humorous side. The Law was rich in farcical fictions, hair-splitting disputations, Latin lingo, and in a mystifying jargon which puzzled and amused the frequenters of the Courts. The Law gave the Elizabethan dramatists a

LEGAL ALLUSIVENESS

mine from which they drew plenty of material, both tragical and comical.

The Law formed a palpable part of William Shakespeare's personal environment. He was bred in a litigious town with a Court of Record, a Court Leet, a Bench of Justices, six local attorneys, and an Assize Town in easy reach. His father made a hobby of litigation, for he was concerned in more than fifty lawsuits in the course of forty years, and figured, in his palmy days, as a purchaser, a tenant, and a mortgagor of lands or houses. He also served as a member of the municipal council, a juror, an assessor of fines, an arbitrator, and as the High Bailiff of his native town. Towards the end of his life he fell into difficulties, which rendered him liable to judgment and execution against his lands and goods, and involved him in a prolonged suit against his mortgagee. William Shakespeare, following his father's example, became a purchaser, a tenant, and a mortgagor of houses and lands, and was interested as a party or a witness in several legal proceedings. Hall's and Holinshed's *Chronicles*, and some of the other sources of his plays, contained stores of information about constitutional problems as well as about crimes, such as treason and their punishment.

Plays were acted and masques were staged at the Inns of Court, among whose members were many regular patrons of the Drama, and several successful dramatists.

Notable law cases were recorded by stenographers and were circulated in pamphlet form. They became the subject of ballads and of gossip in the taverns, which were frequented by men of the stage and of the Law. Dekker, one of Shakespeare's most popular contemporaries, sprinkled a tavern scene with sixteen legal technicalities, fifteen of which occur in Shakespeare's plays, and have been relied upon as evidence of Shakespeare's legal knowledge. They were really no more than illustrations of a passing vogue.

Shakespeare's legal allusions were less numerous and far less technical than those of Ben Jonson and other dramatists of that time. This has been made clear by the industry and research of Mr. J. M. Robertson, who has made a special study of the subject. For example, Ben Jonson in *The Epicene* (iv. 2) introduces *Morose*, who is described as 'a gentleman who does not love Noise'. He complains jestingly of having had to endure in Court 'speaking and counter-speaking, with the several voices of citations, appellations, allegations, certifi-

LEGAL ALLUSIVENESS

cates, attachments, interrogatories, references, convictions and afflictions'. Again, in *The Staple of News*, Ben Jonson brings on the stage, not only a 'Man o' Law' called Picklock, but also four female characters with the following names which are redolent of a lawyer's office—*Mortgage, Statute, Band* and *Wax*. The dramatist makes Picklock boast that he has at his command all the 'cant' of Westminster Hall—'Pleas, Bench and Chancery, Fee Farm, Fee Tail, Tenant in Dower, at Will, for Term of Life, by copy of Court-Roll, Knight service, Homage, Fealty, Escuage, Soccage or Frankalmoyne, Great Sergeanty or Burgage'. There is nothing in any of Shakespeare's plays to equal this torrent of legal tags. Hamlet's speech over the lawyer's skull in the graveyard scene is the nearest approach to it.

Peele, in his play of *Edward I*, introduces into one quip three Writs of a kind seldom mentioned on the modern stage: 'Return your *Habeas Corpus*. Here's a *Certiorari* for your *Procedendo*.' There is nothing like this in Shakespeare, and none of these Writs are even mentioned in his plays. Nashe makes one of his characters suggest to the Devil to issue a Writ of Extent upon the souls of those who had incurred a Writ of Præmunire by introducing 'honest principles' into Hell. The Writ of Extent was the regular Writ of Execution against land. The Writ of Præmunire became a commonplace of Tudor history and of the Elizabethan drama. Almost every dramatist used it in his dialogue. Nobody suggests that Peele or Nashe were lawyers, yet these references are more pungent and precise than any of the kind in Shakespeare. When we find Ben Jonson introducing a 'Court of Love' where witnesses are sworn on Ovid's *De Arte Amandi*, and Dekker staging an Assize Court in Hades, where a jury of brokers are empanelled to try all the villains in Hell, we are obliged to admit that some of the forensic flights of Shakespeare's imagination seem comparatively tame.

LEGAL ALLUSIONS IN ELIZABETHAN POEMS AND SONNETS

It was in their verses and sonnets, even more than in their plays, that the Elizabethan poets made a surprising use of legal jargon and technicality. Edmund Spenser set the example by making Cupid hold a court for the trial of a maiden for murdering her lover by breaking his heart. She is arrested, refuses to plead, and only submits when she has been threatened with the terrible penalty of Peine Forte et Dure.

LEGAL ALLUSIVENESS

Barnabe Barnes makes a lover's heart figure in a variety of legal transactions. It is 'leased', 'pawned', 'bailed', 'mortgaged', and 'disposed of by Deed of Gift'. Finally, the inconstant nymph, who has been the principal party in some of these proceedings, is arraigned and placed upon her trial in the Court of Steadfast Love. Even more extravagant were the sonnets of a poet who used the *nom de plume* of Zepheria. In one of them a lover appeals to a 'Court of Requests' over which his mistress presides as judge in her own cause. He incurs a Writ of Supersedeas, and only escapes a Writ of Præmunire by a prudent submission to the Court.

LEGAL ALLUSIONS IN SHAKESPEARE'S SONNETS

There was less pedantry and less Latin in Shakespeare's poetic legalisms than in those of his contemporaries. In the 30th Sonnet he compares his mind to a tribunal before which he summons Memory as a party or witness. 'Where to the sessions of sweet silent thought I summon up remembrance of things past.' In the 35th Sonnet he takes pride in acting as his friend's advocate against himself, and as his friend's accessory in robbing himself. The 46th Sonnet presents in fanciful phraseology the proceedings in an Action for Partition. The plaintiff is a lover's heart; the defendant is the lover's eye. The property which is to be partitioned is the fair lady who is the object of the lover's passion. The pleadings are sketched romantically, and the jury which is empanelled to try the case is composed of a quest of 'thoughts all tenants to the heart'. By their verdict the lady's 'outward' beauty is apportioned to the eye, and her 'inward love' is allotted to the heart. The imagery in this sonnet was surprisingly juristic, but not more so than in the sonnets of Spenser, Barnabe Barnes, and Zepheria.

THE INNS OF COURT—THE TEMPLE

CHAPTER II

THE INNS OF COURT—THE TEMPLE

THERE were several points of contact in the time of Elizabeth and James I between the Inns of Court and the stage. One of these links was the occasional performance, at the Revels of the Inns of Court, of dramatic masterpieces by companies of professional players. Two Shakespearian comedies are recorded as having been performed in this way during the lifetime of the dramatist. These were the *Comedy of Errors*, which was acted in the Hall of Gray's Inn in December, 1594; and *Twelfth Night*, which was presented in the Hall of the Middle Temple in February, 1602. Another bond of union with the drama was the presence at the Inns of Court of a succession of brilliant dramatists, which included such accomplished playwrights as Francis Beaumont, of the Inner Temple; John Ford, of the Middle Temple;

Thomas Lodge, of Lincoln's Inn; and George Gascoigne, of Gray's Inn. A third link with the stage was the frequent presentations at the Inns of Court of masques and revels, devised and acted by the young lawyers and students. Sometimes it was the custom for the older lawyers to join in dancing round the fireplace in the centre of the Hall. Perhaps, in *Twelfth Night* (i.–3.), Sir Andrew Aguecheek was referring to these convivialities, for the amusement of the Middle Templars, when he said to Sir Toby Belch, 'I delight in masques and revels sometimes altogether.' To Sir Toby's inquiry, 'Art thou good at these kickshawes, Knight?,' Sir Andrew modestly replied that he could 'cut a caper' in a 'gaillard', but he would not compare himself with 'an old man'.

The members of the Inns of Court figured amongst the constant patrons of the drama, and amongst the regular frequenters of the theatre. Their patronage was appreciated by the dramatists. Ben Jonson, in dedicating *Every Man in his Humour* to the Inns of Court, described them as 'the noblest nurseries of humanity and liberty in the Kingdom'. Shakespeare paid them a subtle compliment, when he made it part of Jack Cade's revolutionary programme to 'pull them down' (2 *Henry VI*, iv. 7).

THE TEMPLE

THE TEMPLE

We learn from contemporary evidence that William Shakespeare was a topic of conversation in the Temple. A well-known anecdote about the dramatist and his fellow-actor, Richard Burbage, would not have come down to us if Mr. Towse, a Bencher of the Inner Temple, had not related it to Mr. John Manningham, a student of the Middle Temple, who recorded it in his diary. With the Middle Temple the poet had a direct personal link. His cousin, Thomas Greene, who represented him in the family litigation about John Lambert's mortgage, is generally identified with the Thomas Greene of the Middle Temple, who became a Reader, a Bencher and the Treasurer of that Society.

The dramatist's picture of the social life at the Temple in that age tallies very closely with that of Sir John Fortescue, King Henry VI's Lord Chief Justice, who tells us in his *De Laudibus Legum Angliæ*, written in about 1470, that 'Knights, Barons, and the greatest nobility of the Kingdom often place their children in those Inns of Court, not so much to make the laws their study, much less to live by the profession, having large patrimonies of their own, but to form their manners and to preserve them from the contagion of vice'. The Inns of Court resembled Universities, and their members took pride in them and kept in touch with them in after-life.

PRINCE HAL AT THE TEMPLE

According to Shakespeare, two Princes of the House of Plantagenet and three of the greatest nobles of the fifteenth century were members of the Temple. In the Second Part of *King Henry IV*, Shakespeare indicates that Prince Henry, afterwards Henry V, was a member of the Temple, and that he made himself at home there. When the Prince is on the eve of starting for the front to quell the Percy Rebellion, he names 'the Temple Hall' as his rendezvous with Sir John Falstaff. 'Jack,' says the Prince, 'meet me to-morrow in the Temple Hall at two o'clock in the afternoon. There shalt thou know thy charge and there receive money and order for thy furniture.'

It is not made clear whether Sir John Falstaff was a member of the Temple. We know that he had been a member of Clement's Inn, which was an Inn of Chancery belonging to the Inner Temple, and serving the purpose of a preparatory college for its parent society. Accordingly, if he had pursued the law student's ordinary course of education, he would have proceeded

THE TEMPLE

to the Temple, after completing his studies at Clement's Inn.

PRINCE RICHARD PLANTAGENET AT THE TEMPLE

Richard Plantagenet figures in the First Part of *King Henry VI* (Act II, Sc. 5) as a resident member of the Temple. His uncle, the childless Edward Mortimer, is brought upon the stage, as a dying prisoner in the Tower of London. From his death-bed he sends for his nephew, in order to remind him of the obligations which are about to fall upon him as the heir of the Yorkist title to the Crown, and in order to admonish him to be wary and politic. When he inquires whether his nephew will come, the First Gaoler replies:

> Richard Plantagenet, my Lord, will come.
> We sent into the Temple, unto his chamber,
> And answer was returned that he will come.

A MOOT IN THE GARDEN

Another scene of the same play (Act II, Sc. 4) is staged in the Temple Gardens. Six members of the Society enter the garden from 'the Temple Hall', where they have been 'wrangling' over the dynastic quarrel which is brewing between the Houses of York and Lancaster. Four of them are Yorkists, namely, Richard Plantagenet, Warwick the King-maker, and two lawyers, one of whom is named Vernon. Two of them are Lancastrians, namely, the Earls of Somerset and Suffolk, who were the heads respectively of the noble houses of Somerset and De La Pole. The discussion in the Hall appears to have been a sort of 'moot', and the Earl of Suffolk tells us why the mooters had come out of doors:

> Within the Temple Hall we were too loud.
> The garden here is more convenient.

In the garden the factions fall to high words, and take sides by plucking roses. The Earls of Somerset and Suffolk pluck red roses, Richard Plantagenet, Warwick and the two lawyers pluck white ones. When the Lancastrians have departed in anger, Plantagenet turns to his fellow-Yorkists, and says:

> Come, let us four to dinner: I daresay
> This quarrel will draw blood another day.

Here we are reminded how ancient is the custom at the Inns of Court of dining in messes, each of which consists of four members. In these scenes a glimpse is given of the Inns of Court just as Chief Justice Fortescue painted them. Lawyers are seen mingling with non-legal members of high rank, mooting, dining and using the garden when the season or the nature of the business in hand made it convenient to do so.

THE INNS OF COURT—GRAY'S INN, AND LINCOLN'S INN

CHAPTER III

THE INNS OF COURT—GRAY'S INN, AND LINCOLN'S INN

GRAY'S INN

It is certain that William Shakespeare knew something about the Society of Gray's Inn; and that the Society of Gray's Inn knew something about William Shakespeare. When the dramatist in the Second Part of *King Henry IV* (iii. 2) imagined a pugilistic encounter between a law student and a bruiser of the time, he staged it 'behind Gray's Inn'. When the Society of Gray's Inn presented a comedy in their Hall for the amusement of a brilliant gathering at their Christmas revels of 1594, they selected the *Comedy of Errors*, which was a new play by a young actor-dramatist of thirty years of age—one William Shakespeare. The Records of Lincoln's Inn are comparatively reticent about Plays and Revels. But there is evidence to confirm the tradition that the revels at Lincoln's Inn were as brilliant as those of any of her sister societies. The chief reveller at Lincoln's Inn bore the title of 'Prince De La Grange'.

LORD BURGHLEY

Lord Burghley, Queen Elizabeth's Lord Treasurer, started his career as a lawyer of Gray's Inn, and always remained a loyal and attached member of that Society. For many years he held the Judicial office of Master of the Court of Wards, and he made a habit of admitting to Gray's Inn the young men of rank and fortune who became his Wards of Court. Among them were Lords Oxford, Southampton, and Rutland. He showed wisdom and high purpose in guiding the Queen, who was fortunate in having so prudent and far-seeing an adviser. Ben Jonson made him the subject of a noble eulogy. Shakespeare is said by some ingenious critics to have had Lord Burghley in his mind in the character of Polonius. The suggestion is a plausible one. Polonius's advice to Laertes has much in common with the counsel which Lord Burghley is found giving to one of his sons.

LORD BURLEIGH

A MEMBER OF GRAY'S INN
MASTER OF THE COURT OF WARDS

(*Pages* xxxv, 26, 31)

GRAY'S INN, AND LINCOLN'S INN

THE CHRISTMAS REVELS OF 1594

Of all the revels that were held at the Inns of Court, none were more famous than the Christmas revels of 1594 at Gray's Inn, which extended over a fortnight or more, and were revived at Shrove-tide for the Queen at Greenwich. According to immemorial custom, a Prince was elected from the young members of the Inn with the title of 'Prince of Purpoole', which was the name of the parish in which the Inn was situated. He was also invested with the titles of Archduke, Duke and Marquis of other places in the vicinity. The Prince on this occasion was a youth named Henry Hulme, who was chosen for his skill and activity at revelling and dancing. So important was his position in the eyes of the Court and of the public, that he was entertained by the Lord Mayor and knighted by the Queen in his year of office. The *Comedy of Errors* was played in the Hall on the night of December 28th before a brilliant audience. The Hall was so crowded that, to quote a contemporary record of the proceedings, 'the night was begun and continued to the end in nothing but confusion and errors, whereupon it was ever afterwards called the Night of Errors'.

SHAKESPEARE AND THE LAW

LORD STRANGE AND LORD HUNSDON

It was not surprising that one of Shakespeare's plays should have been acted at Gray's Inn in 1594. One of his earliest engagements was in the company of Lord Strange (afterwards 5th Earl of Derby), who was a member of that Society. In 1594 Lord Strange's company was transferred to the Lord Chamberlain and Shakespeare became one of the Lord Chamberlain's 'servants'. The Lord Chamberlain was Lord Hunsdon, nephew of Anne Boleyn, first cousin of Queen Elizabeth, and a member of Gray's Inn. His coat of arms was seen by a visitor in the seventeenth century emblazoned on one of the windows of the Hall. It was probably by his direction or leave that a play, which was in the repertory of his company of actors, was performed in the Hall of the Inn to which he belonged.

LORD SOUTHAMPTON AND LORD RUTLAND

But there was a participator in the Gray's Inn revels of 1594 who was nearer and dearer to William Shakespeare than either Lord Strange or Lord Hunsdon. This was Henry Wriothesley, 3rd Earl of Southampton, a youth of 20 years of age, to whom the dramatist had dedi-

LORD HUNSDON

A MEMBER OF GRAY'S INN
LORD CHAMBERLAIN TO QUEEN ELIZABETH

(*Page* 33)

GRAY'S INN, AND LINCOLN'S INN

cated his *Venus and Adonis* in 1593 and his *Lucrece* in that very year of 1594. This young man had been admitted to the Inn when he was a boy of 14, and, being an ardent lover of the drama, had taken an interest in the Society's masques and revels. His presence at the Society's entertainments of 1594 is recorded in the official history of those revels.

Southampton was joined at Gray's Inn a few years afterwards by the young Earl of Rutland. They became *habitués* of the theatre and lovers of the drama, and particularly of the drama of Shakespeare, who is believed to have taken them and the other young men of their set as the models which he reproduced upon the stage under such names as Bassanio, Gratiano, Romeo, Benedick, Florizel and Valentine. Southampton and Rutland became the stars of a melodrama of real life. This was Lord Essex's rebellion in 1601. They were seriously implicated in this mad enterprise. Essex was executed for high treason; Southampton was sentenced to death, but his punishment was commuted to imprisonment for life. Rutland was heavily fined. Shakespeare did not abandon his fallen patrons. When Ben Jonson and other dramatists denounced them as conspirators and applauded the Queen for punishing them, Shakespeare preserved an eloquent silence. When Elizabeth died two years afterwards, Shakespeare was the only poet who was publicly reproved for dropping no 'sable tears' to mourn her death. Southampton was in the Tower, and he had no tears to spare for the Queen.

SIR PHILIP SIDNEY

On the walls of Gray's Inn hangs a portrait of one of its members whose writings were among the literary sources which Shakespeare studied and used. This was Sir Philip Sidney, from whom Shakespeare took hints for the form of his sonnets, and for incidents in the plots of several of his plays.[1] Philip Sidney was admitted to Gray's Inn when a mere boy by Lord Burghley. His father, Sir Henry Sidney—thrice Viceroy of Ireland—was already a member of that House. Philip Sidney was a youth who was endowed with a rare combination of noble qualities. After illuminating a decade of Elizabeth's reign, he fell on the battle-field of Zutphen at the age of 32, having already made an outstanding reputation as a poet, soldier and statesman. Edmund Spenser admired and praised his 'devoted spirit', and was leader of a

---

[1] *Love's Labour's Lost, A Midsummer Night's Dream, As You Like it, King Lear,* and *The Tempest.*

SIR PHILIP SIDNEY

A MEMBER OF GRAY'S INN

(*Pages* 29-31)

chorus of contemporary eulogy. His death evoked more than two hundred poetical memorials, and inspired Shelley's word-portrait of:

> Sidney as he fought
> And as he fell, and as he lived and loved,
> Sublimely mild, a spirit without spot

LORD PEMBROKE

William Herbert was Philip Sidney's nephew. He was a boy when the *Comedy of Errors* was produced. Seven years afterwards he succeeded to the Earldom of Pembroke and joined Southampton and Rutland at Gray's Inn. Like them, he became a patron of the dramatists and an admirer of the great dramatic works of his time. The young Earl was disgraced at Court on account of a love affair with Mary Fitton, the maid of honour whose name has been identified by some writers with the 'Dark Lady of the Sonnets'. The identification is a matter of controversy. Some people say that she was not a 'dark lady' but a 'blonde with blue eyes'. However that may be, she was Pembroke's *inamorata*; and Gray's Inn may have helped to bring them together, for Mary Fitton's father and brother were also members of the Society. It was to Lord Pembroke, whom they coupled with his brother, Lord Montgomery, that the Players dedicated the First Folio of Shakespeare's Plays.

THE SHAKESPEARE COAT OF ARMS

The Shakespeare Coat of Arms, which was issued in 1599, was prepared by two Heralds who were members of Gray's Inn. These were Sir William Dethicke, Garter King-of-Arms, and William Camden, Clarenceux King-of-Arms. Dethicke's own escutcheon has been in a window of Gray's Inn ever since his admission in 1587, and can be seen to-day, after three hundred and forty years, looking as fresh as if it had been placed there yesterday. Camden's portrait hangs in the library of Gray's Inn. Nowadays when the King honours an actor or a dramatist, it is usually by the accolade of Knighthood. In Elizabeth's time actors and dramatists gained social distinction by procuring a grant of a coat of arms which made the recipient a 'gentleman'. When the Shakespeare coat of arms was issued, the Earl of Essex was Earl-Marshal and Chief of the Heralds' College. Southampton and Rutland, who were Essex's friends, probably interested themselves in gratifying the ambition of their protégé.

WILLIAM HERBERT, 3RD EARL OF PEMBROKE

A MEMBER OF GRAY'S INN
LORD CHAMBERLAIN TO KING JAMES I

(*Pages* 31-34)

GRAY'S INN, AND LINCOLN'S INN

A FANCIFUL LINK

There remains a curious link between Gray's Inn, Lincoln's Inn and Shakespeare, although it is a link of a very fanciful kind. The four personages to whom the authorship of the Shakespearian plays and poems has been attributed by ingenious writers in recent years belonged to one or other of these two Societies. These four personages were Francis Bacon, Edward De Vere 17th Earl of Oxford,[1] Roger Manners 5th Earl of Rutland,[2] and William Stanley 6th Earl of Derby.[3] Bacon, Oxford and Rutland were members of Gray's Inn—Derby, whose father and brothers were members of Gray's Inn, was himself a member of Lincoln's Inn. They formed, with Lords Southampton and Pembroke, a group of brilliant Elizabethans, who must have heard of William Shakespeare and were on terms of intimacy with each other. Bacon was nephew, and Oxford was son-in-law, of Burghley. Derby was son-in-law of Oxford, and the *Midsummer Night's Dream* was probably produced for his

---

[1] *Shakespeare Identified*, Cecil Palmer, London, 1920.
[2] *Lord Rutland est Shakespeare*, par M. Demblan, Paris, 1913.
[3] *Sous le Masque de William Shakespeare*, par Professeur Lefranc, Paris, 1919.

wedding. Rutland was Southampton's friend. He was at one time engaged to his friend's sister, and ultimately married Pembroke's first cousin. All these theories of authorship have been summarized impartially in a recent book[1] by Professor Connes, of the University of Dijon, who concludes by giving judgment in favour of the orthodox opinion that the real author was William Shakespeare, of Stratford-on-Avon. The present writer is of the same opinion, but he has avoided dabbling in these controversies. Francis Bacon's memory is worshipped at Gray's Inn. His effigy in its entrance Square personifies the *genius loci*. But the idea that he was the author of the Shakespearian writings finds very little support at Gray's Inn. Certainly, if one of that brilliant group—Bacon, Oxford, Rutland, Derby—was author of two of the most famous poems and thirty-seven of the most famous plays of his time, he was wonderfully successful in keeping the secret from the rest.

[1] *The Shakespeare Mystery*, Cecil Palmer, London, 1927.

THE INNS OF CHANCERY—
CLEMENT'S INN

CHAPTER IV

THE INNS OF CHANCERY— CLEMENT'S INN

SIR JOHN FALSTAFF AND JUSTICE SHALLOW OF CLEMENT'S INN

THE Inns of Chancery have long since disappeared. In Shakespeare's day they were places of legal education which were preparatory to the Inns of Court. One of them was Clement's Inn, which was preparatory to the Inner Temple. Shakespeare made two of his comic characters belong to Clement's Inn. These were Sir John Falstaff and Justice Shallow. Justice Shallow, according to Sir Sidney Lee, was 'beyond doubt a reminiscence of' Sir Thomas Lucy of Charlecote, who resided near Stratford-on-Avon and was a Justice of the Peace, a Commissioner of Musters, a strenuous game-preserver, and the introducer of a Bill in Parliament to make the Game Laws more stringent.

SHAKESPEARE AND THE LAW

THE LUCYS OF CHARLECOTE AND THE INNS OF COURT AND CHANCERY

The Lucys of Charlecote were an ancient family who had been armigerous, that is to say entitled to bear an heraldic coat of arms, for at least three centuries. Their coat of arms reflected their Norman origin, because it was adorned with silver luces. Luce was French for 'pike', the fresh-water fish which was as common in the Avon as in the rivers of Normandy. In Burke's *Commoners of England* (iii. 98) several pages are devoted to the pedigree and to the memorials of the Lucy family, from which it appears that, in the reign of Henry IV, two successive heads of the house served in the retinue of John of Gaunt. The Author of the present book has searched the records of admissions to the Inns of Court, and has discovered the names of five Lucys of Charlecote in Tudor times, and three in the reign of James I. In Elizabeth's time they resorted to the Inner Temple, of which Clement's Inn was an *annexe*.

JUSTICE SHALLOW IN THE 'MERRY WIVES'

In the opening scene of *The Merry Wives of Windsor* we find Justice Shallow introduced as a Justice of the Peace, a strenuous game-

CLEMENT'S INN

preserver, and as the representative of an ancient armigerous family with white luces in its coat of arms. Justice Shallow comes to Windsor, accompanied by his cousin Slender, in order to prosecute Sir John Falstaff before the Star Chamber for riot, burglary and deer-stealing. 'Sir Knight,' said Shallow, 'you have beaten my men, killed my deer, and broke into my lodge.' When the Welsh parson, Sir Hugh Evans, strives to make peace, the dialogue proceeds as follows:—

Shallow: Sir Hugh, persuade me not; I will make a Star Chamber matter of it: if he were twenty Sir John Falstaffs, he shall not abuse Robert Shallow, Esquire.
Slender: In the County of Gloucester, Justice of the Peace, and Coram.
Shallow: Ay, cousin Slender, and custalorum.
Slender: Ay, and Rotolorum too; and a gentleman born, master parson, who writes himself in any Bill, warrant, quittance or obligation, armigero.
Shallow: Ay, that I do, and have done any time these three hundred years.
Slender: All his successors gone before him have done it and all his ancestors that come after him.

Then we come to a jesting dialogue about the family coat of arms. Slender refers to the 'dozen white luces'. Shallow says it is an 'old coat'. The Welsh parson, misapplying the word 'luce', remarks that 'a dozen white louses do become an old coat well—it (the louse) is a familiar beast to man and signifies love'. Shallow brings him back to realities by reminding him that the luce is not a louse, but 'a fresh fish'.

JUSTICE SHALLOW IN 'KING HENRY IV'

Justice Shallow figures again in the Second Part of *King Henry IV* as a Commissioner of Musters, a henchman of John of Gaunt, and an ex-law-student of an Inn of Chancery. In his capacity of Commissioner of Musters he receives Sir John Falstaff, who is collecting recruits in the counties through which he passes on his way to the front. Shallow, as Commissioner of Musters, produces for his inspection five wretched recruits who bear the appropriate names of Mouldy, Bullcalf, Shadow, Wart, and Feeble. Sir John Falstaff, in consideration of a bribe of three pounds, corruptly releases Mouldy and Bullcalf, in spite of the protest of Shallow, who declares that they are the 'likeliest men' of the lot.

Then we find Shallow boasting and Falstaff making fun of his connexion with John of Gaunt. Falstaff declares that Shallow 'talks familiarly of "John o' Gaunt" as if he had been a sworn brother to him; and I'll be sworn a ne'er saw him but once in the Tilt-yard; and then he burst his head for crowding among the Mar-

CLEMENT'S INN

shal's men. I saw it and I told John o' Gaunt he beat his own name'. The pun on the word Gaunt suggests that Shallow was a person of a spare figure. So he is described by Sir John Falstaff, who covers him with ridicule, calling him a 'monkey', a 'mandrake' and, in allusion to his coat of arms, an 'old pike', and representing him as having been a forlorn youth who resembled a 'forked radish with a head fantastically carved upon it with a knife', and as having looked as if he had been 'made after supper out of a cheese-paring'.

JUSTICE SHALLOW AND CLEMENT'S INN

Justice Shallow is described by Falstaff as having been a member of Clement's Inn. 'I do remember him (Shallow) at Clement's Inn,' says the Knight, who adds, 'We have heard the chimes at midnight, Master Shallow.' Shallow would have us believe that he had been a rake and a Don Juan who had sowed very wild oats in those days, and he relates how he had fought a celebrated bruiser named Sampson Stockfish 'behind Gray's Inn'.

The lists of admissions to Clement's Inn have not been preserved. But, as has been mentioned, there were, in the Tudor times, five Lucys of Charlecote at the parent Inn of that

SHAKESPEARE AND THE LAW

Society, the Inner Temple. Sir Thomas Lucy's son and two of his grandsons entered Lincoln's Inn, and a third grandson entered Gray's Inn. Possibly Sir Thomas himself never succeeded in rising higher than an Inn of Chancery.

THE DEER-STEALING LEGEND

Why did Shakespeare caricature Sir Thomas Lucy? The explanation depends upon a tradition which lingered in Stratford-on-Avon some eighty or ninety years after Shakespeare's death, and was recorded by the poet laureate, Nicolas Rowe, and by Archdeacon Davies, who was a vicar in Gloucestershire. According to Rowe, the story ran that young Shakespeare had been addicted to deer-stealing from the park of Sir Thomas Lucy, whose activity in prosecuting him forced the young poacher to flit to London. Archdeacon Davies's account of the incident is cloaked in quaintly euphemistic language. According to him, the young poet was 'much given to all unluckiness in stealing venison and rabbits, particularly of Sir Thomas Lucy, who had him oft whipt and sometimes imprisoned, and at last made him fly to his native county to his great advantage'.

Some doubt has been thrown upon this legend by writers who have considered it improbable

CLEMENT'S INN

that a county magistrate of ancient lineage and knightly descent should have served as a model for a country bumpkin like Justice Shallow. These writers also assert that Sir Thomas Lucy's 'deer park' was at a distance from Charlecote. But there was a 'warren' at Charlecote where roe-deer, as well as rabbits and hares, might be found. It may be unusual, but it does not seem to be incredible, that a county magistrate of ancient lineage should be derided by an aggrieved poet as a country bumpkin. The opinion of the vast majority of Shakespearian writers and commentators accords with that of Sir Sidney Lee, who entertained no doubt that the character of Justice Shallow of Clement's Inn was a reminiscence of Sir Thomas Lucy of Charlecote. Local tradition and the internal evidence in the play seem to support that view very strongly.

ALLUSIONS TO CASES AND
LAWYERS OF NOTE—SIR
WILLIAM GASCOIGNE, JUDGE
HALES, AND JUDGE PHESANT

CHAPTER V

ALLUSIONS TO CASES AND LAWYERS OF NOTE — SIR WILLIAM GASCOIGNE, JUDGE HALES, AND JUDGE PHESANT

CHIEF JUSTICE GASCOIGNE AND HENRY V

THERE is no greater figure in the history of the Judicial Bench than Gascoigne. In the time of King Henry IV our judicial system was in the melting-pot. The true relation to each other of the judiciary and executive was as yet unsettled, and there was a danger of the Bench drifting into an attitude of servility towards the Crown. This danger was averted and a nobler direction was given to the traditions and standards of the Judgment-Seat by Sir William Gascoigne, who was a Reader of Gray's Inn in the reign of King Edward III, King's Sergeant in the reign of King Richard II, and became Lord Chief Justice of the King's Bench under King Henry IV. As Chief Justice he set a splendid example of firmness and independence. When the King required him to impose capital punishment without a regular trial upon a prelate and a peer, he replied, 'Neither you, my Lord, nor any of your subjects, can, according to the laws of England, sentence any prelate to death, and the Earl has a right to be tried by his peers.'

Shakespeare, in 2 *King Henry IV*, has immortalized an incident which had been solemnly cited by two of the Judges in Westminster Hall when Sir Robert Catlyne had been Chief Justice of the King's Bench and Sir Robert Whidden a Judge of that Court. The Report[1] runs as follows: 'Whidden vouches a case in the time of Gascoigne, Chief Justice of England, who committed the Prince' (i.e. Prince Hal, afterwards Henry V) 'to prison because he would have taken a prisoner from the Bar of the King's Bench, and he, very submissively obeying him, went thither, according to order; at which the King was rightly rejoiced that he had a judge who dared to minister justice upon his son the Prince, and that he had a son who obeyed him.' Catlyne, C.J., assented. The historical authenticity of this story about

[1] Crompton, *Autorité et Jurisdiction des Courts* (1594), p. 79.

SIR WILLIAM GASCOIGNE

Gascoigne and Prince Hal has been questioned; but it is evident that it rested upon a tradition which was accepted as authentic in Westminster Hall. According to Shakespeare (2 *King Henry IV*, i. 2), the prisoner whom the Prince would have taken from the Bar of the Court was Bardolph, one of Falstaff's boon companions.

Shakespeare gave currency to the story that Henry V, after his accession, re-appointed Gascoigne Chief Justice with a gracious command 'still to bear the balance and the sword'. But history does not confirm this part of the legend. It appears that soon after Henry V's accession Gascoigne either resigned or was superseded. However that may be, Shakespeare rendered a national service by giving a vivid presentation in the person of Sir William Gascoigne, of those qualities of judicial courage and independence which are characteristic of the administration of the criminal law in the British Empire and in the United States.

ALLUSIONS TO CONTEMPORARY LAW AND LAWYERS

Legal proceedings, both criminal and civil, attracted more public attention in the reigns of Elizabeth and James I than they do to-day. The annual infliction of capital punishment in as many as eight hundred cases, on an average, made the administration of the criminal law a grim and never-ending tragedy. A series of notable trials for high treason, such as those of Mary Queen of Scots, the Duke of Norfolk, the Earl of Essex, and Sir Walter Raleigh, created a succession of political sensations. There was plenty of human interest to be extracted from the Cause List of the Star Chamber; and there was much to tickle the fancy of both the initiated and the uninitiated in the fine cobwebs that were weaved, and the quaint jargon that was bandied to and fro in the noisy and crowded courts of Westminster Hall. In the present chapter, and in the following chapters, mention will be made of eight supposed references to cases or lawyers of note which are scattered among the plays of Shakespeare. Two of them have been widely accepted as genuine allusions to well-known legal proceedings. The others stand on a different footing. Three of them have not won their way to general acceptance, but there is enough to be said in their favour to render them deserving of mention and of further investigation. Chapter VII contains three new suggestions which are made by the present author.

JUDGE HALES

THE SAD CASE OF JUDGE HALES

An undoubted allusion to a memorable lawsuit occurs in the churchyard scene in *Hamlet* (v. 1), where the two diggers of Ophelia's grave are discussing the philosophy of suicide. One of the most notable lawsuits of the Elizabethan era had been *Hales* v. *Petit*. It appears, from Plowden's report of the case (at p. 253), that Sir James Hales, a Judge of the Court of Common Pleas, lost his reason and committed suicide by drowning himself in a stream near his home at Canterbury. A coroner's jury having returned a verdict of *felo de se*, Sir James Hales's estates were forfeited to the Crown. His widow brought an action with the object of saving from the forfeiture an estate which she and her husband had held as joint tenants. She claimed that the estate had vested in her as a joint tenant in her husband's lifetime, and that her right of survivorship sprang up immediately after her husband's death, and took priority of the forfeiture. The case was the occasion of some highly sophistical arguments upon the question whether Sir James Hales' felonious act in committing suicide preceded his death in point of time. The arguments upon this quaint question became notorious as constituting a *reductio ad absurdum* of juristic sophistry; and the case lingered for many years in the memory of the legal profession and of the public as the most hair-splitting case of that hair-splitting age.

One extract from the arguments and another from the judgments will suffice for the purpose of their comparison with Shakespeare's parody. Sergeant Walshe, for the defendants, submitted that 'the act of self-destruction consists of three parts. The first is the imagination, which is a reflexion or meditation of the man's mind whether or no it be convenient to destroy himself and in what way it may be done; the second is the resolution, which is a determination of the mind to destroy himself and to do it in this or that particular way; the third is the perfection, which is the execution of what the mind has resolved to do. And this perfection consists of two parts, viz. the beginning and the end. The beginning is the doing of that act which causes the death, and the end is the death, which is only a sequel of the act. Then, here the act of Sir James Hales, which is evil and the cause of his death, is the throwing of himself in the water, and the death is but the sequel thereof.' The following was the sage judgment which Judge Browne delivered from the Bench: 'Sir

JUDGE HALES

James Hales was dead. And how came he by his death? It may be answered, by drowning. And who drowned him? Sir James Hales. And when did he drown him? In his lifetime. So that Sir James Hales being alive caused Sir James Hales to die, and the act of the living was the death of the dead man. And for this offence it is reasonable to punish the living man, who committed the offence, and not the dead man.'

Now let us turn to Shakespeare's parody. Ophelia, like Sir James Hales, had lost her reason and had committed suicide by drowning. Over her grave the first gravedigger propounds to his colleague the question whether she ought to have a Christian burial. His comrade, in a law-abiding spirit, says 'yes', because the 'coroner' had sat on her and had found it so. The first gravedigger is not satisfied with the 'crowner's' law. He subdivides the subject in a vein which was intended to parody the subdivisions of the subject in Sergeant Walshe's argument in *Hales* v. *Petit*. 'For here lies the point: If I drown myself wittingly it argues an act: and an act hath three branches; it is to act, to do, to perform; argal she drowned herself wittingly.' He then indulges in a travesty of the reasoning of that learned pundit, Judge

SHAKESPEARE AND THE LAW

Browne. 'Here lies the water: good; and here stands the man: good. If the man goes to the water and drowns himself, it is will he, nill he, he goes—mark you that; but if the water come to him and drown him, he drowns not himself; argal, he that is not guilty of his own death shortens not his own life.'

There can be no reasonable doubt that, when the dramatist penned this scene, he had in his mind the sophistries which had given an enduring notoriety to the case of *Hales* v. *Petit*.

PETER PHESANT, ADVOCATE

The *Winter's Tale* (iv. 3) contains a mysterious collocation of the words 'advocate' and 'pheasant', which has baffled the critics, and has induced more than one of them to suggest that there is a mistake in the Folio of 1623, and that the word 'present' should be substituted for 'pheasant'. The passage occurs in a dialogue between three comic characters, Autolycus, a Clown, and a Shepherd. The Shepherd tells Autolycus that he is seeking an audience with the King—Autolycus asks, 'What advocate hast thou?' The Clown observes, 'Advocate is a word for pheasant, say you have none.' The Shepherd replies, 'I have no pheasant cock nor hen.' Here we have a perplexing puzzle of

JUDGE PHESANT

which the following explanation has been suggested as a possible key. There was a notable family of advocates of the name of Phesant who were conspicuous at Gray's Inn and in the Courts in the sixteenth and seventeenth centuries. Peter Phesant the elder was Reader of Gray's Inn in 1582 and afterwards became the Queen's Attorney-General in the North. His son, Peter Phesant the younger, was called to the Bar at Gray's Inn in 1608. He attained a rapid success and ultimately became a Judge of the Court of Common Pleas. The probable date of the production of *Winter's Tale* was 1611. The elder Phesant had died recently and the younger Phesant was a junior member of the Bar. The father's name was familiar to the public and the son was following him in the advocate's profession in which he was winning his way to distinction. Thus the collocation of the words 'advocate' and 'pheasant' is explainable without any emendation of the text of the First Folio.

ALLUSIONS TO CASES AND
LAWYERS OF NOTE—SIR
EDWARD COKE, SIR TOBY
AND SIR HOBY, AND CHIEF
BARON MANWOOD

CHAPTER VI

ALLUSIONS TO CASES AND LAWYERS OF NOTE—SIR EDWARD COKE, SIR TOBY AND SIR HOBY, AND CHIEF BARON MANWOOD

SIR ANDREW AGUECHEEK AND SIR EDWARD COKE

SIR EDWARD COKE was a learned lawyer and a courageous advocate. But he had the defects of these qualities. The study of the Law monopolized his mind to such a degree as to breed in him a contempt for the lighter fields of wit and wisdom. He derided poets as 'fools' and actors as 'vagrants'. He denounced the Stage in unmeasured terms; and Shakespeare is believed to have revenged his tribe by lampooning Sir Edward in *Twelfth Night*.

In 1603 Sir Edward Coke, as Attorney-General, conducted the prosecution of Sir Walter Raleigh for High Treason. Raleigh, who was a member of the Middle Temple, was accused of complicity with Lord Cobham and others in a treasonable plot. The case for the Crown was a shadowy one. The historian, Samuel Gardiner, tells us that 'a century later Raleigh might well have smiled at the evidence which was brought against him'. Coke made up for the want of proof by the terrible violence of his vituperation.

To 'thou' an inferior or a prisoner was a common mode of conveying contempt or insult. The Attorney-General overwhelmed Raleigh with volleys of contemptuous 'thous'. 'Thou art a monster,' 'Thou are the most vile and execrable traitor that ever lived,' 'I want sufficient words to express thy viperous treason,' 'Thou are an odious fellow, thy name is hateful to all the realm of England for thy pride,' 'I will now make it appear that there never lived a viler viper upon the face of the earth than thou.' These were some of his flowers of rhetoric. When he was enlarging upon Lord Cobham's guilt, Raleigh exclaimed, 'What is that to me?' Coke retorted by 'thouing' him thrice: 'All that Lord Cobham did was by thy instigation, thou viper; I thou thee, thou traitor.' After the trial Coke incurred criticism for having thou'd Raleigh in such a scandalously

SIR WALTER RALEGH

A MEMBER OF THE MIDDLE TEMPLE

(*Pages* 50, 60-62)

violent way from behind the shelter of his professional privilege.

Coke's 'thouing' of Raleigh was parodied by Shakespeare in *Twelfth Night* (iii. 2 and 4), where Sir Toby Belch urges Sir Andrew Aguecheek to challenge Cesario to a duel, and, in doing so, to call his enemy a 'rogue' and a 'villain'. In particular he admonishes him thus: 'If thou thou'*st* him some thrice, it shall not be amiss.' Sir Andrew accordingly composes a challenge, the vigorous terms of which fully justify him in declaring, 'I warrant there's vinegar and pepper in it.' That it contained more pepper than proof appears from the following passage: 'Whatsoever thou art, thou art but a scurvy fellow—Wonder not . . . why I do call thee so, for I will show thee no reason for 't.' Finally, Sir Andrew is congratulated by his hearers upon sending a challenge which is 'good and valiant' and nevertheless keeps 'o' the windy side of the law', 'for it comes to pass oft, that a terrible oath, with a swaggering accent sharply twanged off, gives manhood more approbation than ever proof itself would have earned him.'

Twelfth Night first appeared in print in the Folio of 1623, but we know that it had been produced in the Middle Temple Hall as early as 1602. This passage, if it refers to the trial of Raleigh, must have been interpolated into the play after its first production. We have several instances of such interpolations in the Shakespearian plays, and it is probable that this is an instance of the kind.

SIR TOBY AND SIR HOBY

There are some other scenes in *Twelfth Night* where Sir Toby Belch and his boon-companions create a disturbance in Olivia's house by their revelry, and by the noisy way in which they turn the Puritan steward Malvolio into ridicule. It is highly probable that these scenes cover an allusion to a sensational dispute between Sir Posthumus Hoby and William Eure, son of Lord Eure, which occupied the Star Chamber in 1601, a few months before the production of *Twelfth Night* in the Hall of the Middle Temple. Both Hoby and Eure were members of Gray's Inn. Hoby was a nephew of Lord Burghley.

It appears from the proceedings (which are preserved in the Public Record Office) that Sir Posthumus Hoby was a Puritan who went to reside in Yorkshire. He made enemies in his new environment by his officious activities, which included the ferreting of alleged Popish recusants. His unpopularity among his neighbours seems to afford an explanation of the

SIR TOBY AND SIR HOBY

strange conduct of a party of visitors who stayed in his house under the leadership of William Eure. Hoby complained to the Star Chamber that they misbehaved themselves by upsetting Lady Hoby's household, by playing cards in spite of Hoby's protest, by disturbing family prayers, and otherwise by their riotous and disorderly behaviour. Numerous witnesses made lengthy depositions, and the case was one of the *causes célèbres* of that time.

It is probable that these proceedings were alluded to in the scenes referred to above, in which Sir Toby Belch and his fellows are represented as keeping late and disorderly hours in Olivia's house, and as making the Puritan steward Malvolio the target of their pranks. The coincidence of date, the common features of the baiting of a Puritan and of the disturbance of a Lady's household, and the jingling similarity between the names 'Hoby' and 'Toby' lend colour to the suggestion. It should be noted that in the Star Chamber Sir Hoby was the aggrieved party, while in the play Sir Toby was the aggressor.

'THE COMEDY OF ERRORS' AND CHIEF BARON MANWOOD

A remarkable personage of the Elizabethan

period was Sir Roger Manwood, a member of the Inner Temple. Manwood was a favourite among the Templars. He had taken part, when a student, in the revels, over which Lord Robert Dudley (afterwards Earl of Leicester) presided. On that occasion, Manwood had filled the mock office of 'Lord Chief Baron of the Exchequer'. Eighteen years afterwards he was appointed to that very office and became a real Lord Chief Baron of the Exchequer. He was an energetic and popular personage, who in private life bore the reputation of being kind-hearted and benevolent. In his judicial office, however, he seems to have acted in a very arbitrary and high-handed manner.

Chief Baron Manwood was the central figure of a sensational case about a gold chain which made a great stir in the Star Chamber in the years 1591 and 1592. Hearing that his son had disposed of a gold chain to a goldsmith named Underwood, he sent for the goldsmith and terrified him into handing over the chain, which he put into his pocket and refused to give back. The goldsmith complained to the Star Chamber, with the result that the episode made a noise in Westminster Hall, of which the *Comedy of Errors* is supposed by some commentator to have contained an echo.

CHIEF BARON MANWOOD

A letter from the Privy Council addressed to Manwood, in terms of stern admonishment, is preserved in the Public Record Office. The Council wrote to the Chief Baron that they were satisfied 'upon the oath of divers persons' that 'the said chaine was bought lawfullie in open market, and that likewise you got the chaine into your hands by means of threatening speeches used by you unto the said Underwood to send him to the Marshalsea, having purposelie a Marshal's man by you with a tipstaff in his hand, whereby the poor suppliant was terrified and chose rather to deliver the chaine to you than to endure the charges and other inconveniences of imprisonment'. The Council went on to censure the Lord Chief Baron's conduct as unworthy of a Judge of his 'place and learning', and in their opinion 'a verie foule example and slanderous to the rest of his calling.' They required him to 'deliver up the chaine or the value thereof' to Underwood, or in the alternative to 'appear before the Council and answer for his refusal'. The Lord Chief Baron proved refractory, and was confined to his house by order of the Council until he apologized and made submission.

Soon after the occurrence of this sensational case the *Comedy of Errors* was written. It was acted, as we know, in Gray's Inn Hall in 1594 at the Christmas revels. One of the entanglements of the plot, which turned upon the resemblance between two sets of twin brothers, was the mistaken delivery of a gold chain to one of a pair of twins by a goldsmith of Ephesus. Out of this incident sprang a series of misunderstandings, including an accusation and an arrest. The germ of the incident came from Plautus's *Menæchmi*, but Shakespeare worked it up in his own masterly fashion. The fancy of an audience at Gray's Inn in 1594 would have been tickled by a covert allusion to the then recent *cause célèbre* of *Underwood* v. *Manwood*.

SIR ROGER MANWOOD

A MEMBER OF THE INNER TEMPLE
LORD CHIEF BARON OF THE EXCHEQUER

(*Pages* 63-66)

ALLUSIONS TO CASES AND LAWYERS OF NOTE— SHELLEY'S CASE, FINES AND RECOVERIES, AND THE CASE OF PERPETUITIES

CHAPTER VII
ALLUSIONS TO CASES AND LAWYERS OF NOTE— SHELLEY'S CASE, FINES AND RECOVERIES, AND THE CASE OF PERPETUITIES

SHELLEY'S CASE

The technical meaning of the words 'purchase' and 'purchased,' in the law of real property, had become familiar to the public in Shakespeare's time. Lands were deemed by the Law to come to a person by 'purchase' or to be 'purchased', when they were acquired by him by some other title than by descent, and the person who thus acquired them was called a 'purchaser'. These technical phrases constantly cropped up in the arguments in Shelley's Case, which was a *cause célèbre* (1579–81) when Shakespeare was a youth, and has been a Leading Case ever since. Recently the Rule in Shelley's Case was abolished by Lord Birkenhead's Law of Property

Act, and it does not apply to instruments taking effect after 1925. But during the interval of nearly three centuries and a half, which divided the time of Sir Edward Coke from the time of Lord Birkenhead, the 'Rule in Shelley's Case' has frequently been used both by lawyers and by laymen as a stock-phrase to describe a highly technical enunciation of the Law by a Judicial Tribunal. Sir Edward Coke was counsel in the case, and he tells us in the first volume of his Reports[1] that 'such was the rareness and difficulty' of Shelley's case that it was 'generally known', and he adds that it was on this account that, after it had been argued at length before the Court of Queen's Bench, the Queen directed the Lord Chancellor to assemble all the Judges of England to give judgment upon it. The case largely turned upon the distinction between estates taken by 'purchase' and estates taken by 'inheritance' or 'descent' and between words of 'limitation' and words of 'purchase'. These phrases, contrasting the legal meaning of 'purchase' with the opposite idea of inheritance or descent, occurred about a hundred times in Coke's Report of Shelley's Case.

Shelley's Case made the legal meaning of

[1] Part I, 105 c.

SHELLEY'S CASE

the word 'purchased' so familiar to the public that Shakespeare used it loosely where he wished to distinguish acquisition of property or of qualities by inheritance from acquisition of them in some other way. When Henry IV on his death-bed reminds his son that the crown which 'in me was *purchased* falls upon thee in a more fairer sort' (2 *Henry IV*, iv. 4), he means that the crown had come to himself by usurpation, but that his son will take it by descent.[1] When Cæsar, in *Antony and Cleopatra* (i. 4.), describes Antony as an abstract of all faults, Lepidus excuses him by saying that he cannot exchange his faults because they came to him by heredity. The way he puts it is that Antony's faults are 'hereditary rather than *purchas'd*'. Shakespeare's easy application of this very technical notion has naturally surprised some of the commentators; but Coke's statement that Shelley's Case was 'generally known' suggests an obvious explanation. A phrase which seems recondite to us may have been quite intelligible to a theatrical audience in Shakespeare's time, because its technical meaning had been frequently and recently discussed in a *cause célèbre*.

---

[1] Shakespeare's application of the word is happy but loose. Strictly speaking, 'usurpation' did not rank as a 'purchase', *Co. Litt.*, 186.

SHAKESPEARE AND THE LAW

ESTATES TAIL AND FINES AND RECOVERIES

Fines and Recoveries were the quaint devices by which the *Statute de Donis Conditionalibus* (sometimes called the *Statute of Entail*) was circumvented. The Statute contemplated land being tied up indefinitely by means of estates tail. But the Courts set their face against a system which was contrary to public policy because it tended to restrict the free transfer of landed property. Ultimately, the Judges gave their sanction to a device which had the effect of driving a coach and four through the provisions of the Statute of Entail by enabling a tenant in tail to 'bar' (or 'cut off') the entail and to convert his estate into a fee simple by 'suffering a feigned recovery'. Under certain statutes a similar result might be effected by 'levying a fine'. The suffering of a recovery (with a single or a double voucher) was a ludicrous proceeding of a collusive kind in which the Court crier played the leading part of 'common vouchee'. The levying of a fine was an equally farcical proceeding which culminated in something in the nature of a collusive compromise. It enabled estates to be sold free from dower and other burdens. After the tenant in tail had suffered a recovery and had

FINES AND RECOVERIES

levied a fine, his position as owner in fee simple with complete power of alienation became impregnably secure.

The history of the law on this subject had begun with a series of decisions which culminated in Taltarum's Case (1472). The conveyancers tried to circumvent *Taltarum's Case*, but their efforts were defeated in another series of cases, several of which occupied the Courts while Shakespeare was producing his plays. One of the last of them was *Mary Portington's Case* in 1613. In this line of cases the Judges disposed of seven separate contrivances which were invented by ingenious conveyancers with the object of preventing the operation of a 'Recovery'.[1] But the Judges held all these expedients to be ineffectual. The later stages of this prolonged forensic campaign occupied the Courts in Shakespeare's time, and there were few proceedings more familiar to litigants and to frequenters of the Courts than Fines and Recoveries.

What made Fines and Recoveries particularly

---

[1] It was sought to defeat a 'recovery' by means of (1) a condition, (2) a limitation, (3) a custom, (4) a recognisance, (5) a statute, (6) a proviso for forfeiture on attempting to alien, and (7) an agreement not to suffer a recovery. All these artifices were rejected by the Courts.

palatable to a theatre audience was their comicality. The farcicality of these feigned proceedings was so notorious that we find Shakespeare introducing them three times into comic scenes. Unless they had been notorious, the allusions would have had no point for the audience. In the *Merry Wives of Windsor* (iv. 2), when one of the merry wives wishes to give some idea of the utter profligacy of Sir John Falstaff, she speaks of the Devil having him in fee simple, 'with fine and recovery'. In the *Comedy of Errors* (ii. 2) Dromio of Syracuse refers to the difficulty which is experienced by a man, who has the misfortune to be bald by nature, if he desires to 'recover' his hair. Antipholus asks, 'May he not do it by *fine* and *recovery?*' 'Yes,' says Dromio, 'to pay a *fine* for a peruke, and *recover* the lost hair of another man.' Hamlet, in the churchyard scene (v. 1), in the speech over the supposed lawyer's skull, fires off a volley of puns on the same subject: 'Is this the *fine* of his *fines*, and the recovery of his recoveries, to have his *fine* pate full of *fine* dirt?' There is no legal subtlety in these jests. Technical phraseology of this kind, when sufficiently quaint and current, has contributed, in every age, to the 'patter' with which low comedians catch

THE CASE OF PERPETUITIES

laughter from the pit and gallery. Sir Arthur Underhill has pointed out that these references seem very abstruse to us because they have become archaic and unfamiliar. But, in Shakespeare's day the levying of fines and the suffering of recoveries were of everyday occurrence, and the Courts were frequently occupied with cases about them If they had not been so, these jokes and puns could have had no meaning for Shakespeare's public.

THE CASE OF PERPETUITIES (1595)[1]

After the Statute of Entail had been circumvented by Fines and Recoveries, the conveyancers adopted other devices for tying up property perpetually. One of these devices was the creation of 'successive contingent remainders by way of use' under the Statute of Uses. This device was held to be ineffectual in Chudleigh's Case, reported in Coke's Reports.[2] Coke called it 'The Case of Perpetuities', and it was the first case in the law-books in which the word 'perpetuity' occurs. The case lingered in the Court of King's Bench for six years, and was finally argued before all the Judges of England,

---

[1] The Author of this book contributed the Article on *Perpetuities* to Lord Halsbury's *Laws of England*.
[2] Coke's Reports, Part I, 119B.

who gave their decision of 1595. In 1595, or within a year or two afterwards, *All's Well That Ends Well* was written and produced under the name of *Love's Labour's Won*. It appears to have been revived with alterations and additions about 1605 or 1606; and it ultimately appeared in print in the First Folio of 1623. In that play (iv. 3.) Parolles, when he is asked whether Captain Dumain is a person whom gold will corrupt, replies (in a passage already cited) that the Captain for a trifle will 'sell the fee-simple of his salvation', and 'cut the *entail* from all *remainders*, and a *perpetual* succession for it *perpetually*'. This passage looks like a topical allusion to the '*Case of Perpetuities*' which had been so recently decided. At the time when the play was produced, the technical phrases 'entail', 'remainder' and 'perpetuity' had been bandied about in the Courts for six years, and this allusion to them would be likely to be keenly appreciated by audiences which were largely drawn from the legal profession. The subject was further ventilated in the Courts in several subsequent cases. One of them was *Corbet's Case*, which was decided in 1599 and was the second case in the law-books in which the word 'perpetuity' occurs.

SIR EDWARD COKE

A MEMBER OF THE INNER TEMPLE
LORD CHIEF JUSTICE OF THE KING'S BENCH

(*Pages* 59-62, 70, 71, 75)

THE CASE OF PERPETUITIES

The suggestions in the present chapter connecting Shakespeare's use of the words *'purchased'* with Shelley's Case, of *'Fines and Recoveries'* with the contemporary Case Law of his time, and *'remainder'*, *'perpetual'* and *'perpetually'* with the *Case of Perpetuities*, are, so far as the present author knows, entirely new, and he respectfully submits them for the consideration of his brother lawyers.

ALLUSIONS TO COURTS AND PROCEDURE

CHAPTER VIII
ALLUSIONS TO COURTS AND PROCEDURE

JUDGES AND ARBITRATORS

IT is evident that Shakespeare had learned—perhaps as a litigant, or witness, or as a visitor to the Courts—the courtesies of Bench and Bar. He makes 'Judge' Escalus refer to 'Judge' Angelo as 'my brother', and Sir John Falstaff address Chief Justice Gascoigne as 'Your Lordship'. He presents us with a picture of a good judge in Lord Say, who could claim to have maintained the king, the realm and the people, and to have suffered 'sickness and disease' by 'long sitting to determine poor men's causes' (2 *Henry VI*, iv. 7). When he used the office of Judge or Arbitrator in a figurative sense, it was generally to express some impressive idea such as 'Time' or 'Death'. For him Time was the 'old justice that examines offenders', and 'the old common arbitrator'. Death was the 'arbitrator of despair'.

THE GRAND JURY AND THE PETTY JURY

Shakespeare may have seen the Grand Jury sworn at Warwick assizes. He makes Sir Toby Belch declare that Judgment and Reason have been 'Grand jury-men since before Noah was a sailor' (*Twelfth Night*, iii. 2). When Falstaff waylaid some country gentlemen, one of the sarcastic gibes which he hurled at them was, 'You are grand-jurors, are ye? We'll jure ye, i' faith' (1 *Henry IV*, ii. 2). When Dogberry dismisses the constables of his watch, he administers to them the Grand Jurors' oath, 'Keep your fellows' counsel and your own' (*Much Ado About Nothing*, iii. 3). The poet was not blind to the imperfections of the 'great palladium', for he puts the following *dictum* into Judge Angelo's mouth: 'The Jury, passing on the prisoner's life, may, in the sworn twelve, have a thief or two guiltier than him they try' (*Measure for Measure*, ii. 1).

LITIGANTS, WITNESSES, AND ADVOCATES

Shakespeare alludes to litigants ('Plaintiff', 'Defendant', and 'Appellant') as well as to witnesses and to their Oath. He refers to 'Pleas'

SIR WILLIAM GASCOIGNE

A MEMBER OF GRAY'S INN
LORD CHIEF JUSTICE OF THE KING'S BENCH

(*Pages* 47, 49, 81, 103, 106)

COURTS AND PROCEDURE

and 'Pleadings', not in their technical sense, but in the sense of advocacy. He never speaks of a 'barrister', or of a 'Sergeant' in the sense of a coifed barrister. For him the members of the Bar were 'Counsellors' or 'Learned Counsel in the Law', and 'Sergeants' were peace officers. The principal law officer of the Crown was referred to by him as 'the King's Attorney'. When the Duke of York in *King Richard II* (ii. 1) speaks of Hereford's 'Attornies-General', he means his general law agents.

Shakespeare sometimes spoke of lawyers romantically. Pisanio is called 'Love's Counsellor'; Desdemona encouraged Cassio to be merry, 'for thy solicitor shall rather die than give thy cause away'. We meet with such phrases as 'Heart's attorney', 'Attorney of my love'. Indeed, 'Attorney' was his favourite name for a professional pleader in the Court of Love. Twice he advises a litigant, who proposes to plead before that uncertain tribunal, to 'have no attorney but himself'. Only once does he refer disparagingly to the attorney's profession, when he makes Edward IV's Queen (*King Richard III*, iv. 4) describe a flood of idle words as 'windy attorneys to their client woes'. In such phrases as 'die by attorney', the word is used in a non-legal sense of 'proxy' or 'agent'.

SHAKESPEARE AND THE LAW

OFFICERS OF JUSTICE

The plays contain plenty of allusions to officers of justice such as registrars under the name of *registers, notaries,* affeerors, who *affeered* (i.e. settled) amercements or assessments, escheaters under the name of *cheaters, peace officers, constables, scriveners, bailiffs, process-servers,* apparitors (under the name of *paritors*), who were the process-servers of the Ecclesiastical Courts, and *court criers.*

Two examples will serve to illustrate his way of handling such personages. He makes the ravished Lucrece speak of Night as the 'dim register and notary of shame', and in the *Merry Wives of Windsor* (v. 5), he compares the starting of a fairy revel to the opening of a Court of Assize. The fairy Hobgoblin figures as Crier of the Court; and is ordered to open the revels as if it were an Assize: 'Crier Hobgoblin make the fairy o-yes.'

THE WAYS AND HABITS OF THE BAR

Shakespeare had observed the spirit of comradeship of the Bar. In the *Taming of the Shrew* (i. 2), a pair of rival swains are advised not to quarrel, but to do as 'adversaries do in law,' 'strive mightily but eat and drink as friends'. He realized the significance, from

COURTS AND PROCEDURE

the point of view both of lawyer and client, of a fair wage. When King Lear (i. 4) tells his Court Fool that his chatter amounts to 'nothing', the Fool retorts, 'Then 'tis like the breath of an unfee'd lawyer.' On the other hand, Venus complains, when Adonis rejects her, that 'her pleading hath deserved a greater fee'. Only once do we meet with the profession of the Bar in a disreputable atmosphere. When Mistress Overdone, the Viennese panderess (*Measure for Measure*, i, 2), protests against the pulling down of her house, and asks, 'What shall become of me?' her servant comforts her by saying, 'Come; fear not you: good counsellors lack no clients.' The dramatist makes Falstaff count time (as befits an old spendthrift) by the four terms of the legal year, and by the period occupied in an action of debt. Counting time in this way crops up frequently in the plays of that day.

INTERLOCUTORY PROCEEDINGS

In Shakespeare's time it was quite common for a defendant to be arrested upon *mesne process*, and to be imprisoned in default of bail, although no judgment or decision had yet been given against him. In the *Comedy of Errors* (iv. 2)—a play which was first produced at an Inn of Court to amuse a legal audience—

we find Dromio of Syracuse comparing the peace officer who arrests his master upon *mesne process* to a devil who 'before the judgment, carries poor souls to hell'. The arrest is made in an action 'on the case'. This was a class of action to which the old conventional writs of summonses were inapplicable. Accordingly a special writ, analogous to the old writ of trespass, was issued to meet the particular circumstances of each case. Arrests on *mesne process* and actions on the case have little more than an historical interest for the modern lawyer, but they were of frequent occurrence in Shakespeare's day.

Interrogatories were commonly administered to witnesses in judicial proceedings in Shakespeare's time. In the Public Record Office an immense variety of interrogatories are collected, with the witnesses' answers attached. Shakespeare himself gave evidence by means of answering interrogatories. Very interesting are the interrogatories which were administered in the suit of *Mountjoy* v. *Bellot*, in which Shakespeare was a witness. Any visitor to the Public Record Office can peruse the original list of interrogatories with Shakespeare's signed answer. When Portia in the *Merchant of Venice* (v. 1) proposes that she and Nerissa shall make a clean breast of all their machinations, she suggests to Bassanio and Gratiano that they shall 'charge us there upon intergatories, and we will answer all things faithfully'. Gratiano assents, and begins by administering an interrogatory to Nerissa. We refrain from quoting it, because it was somewhat indiscreet.

NONSUIT

A plaintiff was said to be 'nonsuited' when the Court dismissed his case summarily on the ground that upon his own showing he had failed to establish any legal cause of action. The play of *Othello* (i. 1) contains a happy use of this expression. Iago is complaining that the solicitations on his behalf of the great ones of Venice had been rejected by Othello in too summary a fashion. Shakespeare makes him say that the Moor '*nonsuits* my mediators'. Lord Campbell has quoted this passage as 'a striking instance of Shakespeare's proneness to legal phraseology'. But there was nothing surprising about it. The word 'nonsuit' had passed into literary use as a figure of speech which was applicable to the summary rejection of a lover's suit, or to any enterprise that was rudely balked. Similarly, in this passage, Shakespeare applied it to the rejection of a place-hunter's petition.

ALLUSIONS TO CROWN, CRIMINAL, CONSTITUTIONAL AND FEUDAL LAW

CHAPTER IX

ALLUSIONS TO CROWN, CRIMINAL, CONSTITUTIONAL AND FEUDAL LAW

SHAKESPEARE makes numerous allusions to Crown, Criminal, and Constitutional Law, sometimes in the narrative of his plays, sometimes in a metaphorical manner.

ARREST

The Elizabethan poets sometimes applied the idea of Arrest figuratively to a tragical situation, for example, to Death, which was compared by more than one of them to a stern constable, who, sooner or later, makes a prisoner of every man, and never consents to Bail.

The majority of these figures of speech have become hackneyed or are forgotten, but some of Shakespeare's are still remembered and admired. Such a one is the couplet which describes how Lucrece's brother was silenced by the contemplation of his sister's shame. 'The deep vexation of his inward soul' was said to have 'serv'd a dumb arrest upon his tongue'. Another passage survives to our time as a model of tragical simplicity—namely, Hamlet's dying words: 'This fell Sergeant, Death, is strict in his arrest.'

A pedantic commentator made a declivitous descent from the sublime to the ridiculous, when he gravely suggested that Shakespeare must have drawn this simile from his experiences as an Attorney's Clerk in the due execution of writs of *capias ad satisfaciendum*.

CRIMES AND CRIMINAL PROCESS

We find references in the plays to indictments, arraignments, challenges, pleas of guilty and not guilty, convictions and acquittals. Such topics naturally occur here and there both in works of history and of fiction. Shakespeare has been criticized somewhat pedantically for having made Queen Katherine 'challenge' Cardinal Wolsey as her Judge. A critic, well versed in the practice of the 'Old Bailey', was horrified at the suggestion that a prisoner could challenge a judge as distinguished from a juror. But in Queen Katherine's case, the rules of the canon law came into play; and it was historically true

THE COURT OF KING'S BENCH
IN THE TIME OF THE PLANTAGENETS

(*Page* 47)

CRIMINAL LAW

that she 'challenged' Wolsey, at all events in the popular sense of that word.

We meet with plenty of references to crimes. Sometimes they are humorous ones. In *Much Ado About Nothing* (iv. 2) Dogberry betrays a comical ignorance of the difference between perjury and burglary. In the Second Part of *King Henry VI* (iv. 2) Jack Cade promises the proletariat to 'make it felony to drink small beer'. Crimes are sometimes introduced figuratively, as when Desdemona reproaches herself with having 'indicted' Othello 'falsely' and with having 'suborned' her own soul as a witness against him (*Othello*, iii. 3).

PEINE FORTE ET DURE

Peine forte et dure was a punishment which was inflicted upon a prisoner who, when arraigned for a felony, stood mute and refused to plead. The prisoner was laid on his back and, if he persisted in his refusal to speak, was 'pressed to death' by heavy weights. Men sometimes endured pressing to death, for refusing to plead guilty or not guilty, in order to save their families from the ruinous forfeitures which were consequent upon a conviction for felony. This penalty for refusal to speak was too tragical to be overlooked by the dramatists. Shakespeare seems to allude to it figuratively in at least four places. In *Measure for Measure* (v. 1) Lucio compares a degrading marriage to the torture of 'pressing to death'. In *King Richard II* (iii. 4) the unhappy Queen describes herself as 'press'd to death through want of speaking'. In *Much Ado About Nothing* (iii. 1) Hero says that she dare not tell Beatrice that Benedick loves her—because 'If I should speak she'd . . . press me to death with wit'. In *Troilus and Cressida* (iii. 2) Pandarus, having brought the lovers together, promises to show them a bed, and bids them 'because it shall not speak' of their 'pretty encounters, press it to death'.

WAGER OF BATTLE

Wager of Battle (sometimes called Ordeal of Battle) was a mode of trial resorted to in certain classes of cases, particularly in accusations of treason or felony. The case was decided by a personal combat between the parties, or in some instances between their champions. The accused person, if defeated, was liable to be sentenced to death by hanging, and an undecided fight left him liable to be tried by indictment. If the Appellant (i.e. the accuser) yielded, the Appellee (i.e. the accused person) was free. Trials of this kind naturally collected crowds

CRIMINAL LAW

and excited general interest. In the reign of Elizabeth there was a case of wager of battle fought out in public before the Judges of the Common Pleas.

Such a picturesque procedure lent itself to dramatic treatment; Shakespeare introduces it twice. In *King Richard II* (i. 3) the Dukes of Hereford and Norfolk meet in Wager of Battle at Coventry, but the King stops the fight by throwing down his warder. In the Second Part of *King Henry VI* (i. 3) an armourer is accused of high treason by his apprentice. The Duke of Gloucester orders a day to be appointed for single combat in a convenient place; and when the apprentice tries to excuse himself on the ground that he cannot fight, the Duke declares that he 'must fight or else be hanged'. The armourer is defeated in the combat, and confesses his treason before he dies from his wounds.

Lord Campbell fancied that he had found a reference to Wager of Battle in the *Taming of the Shrew* (ii. 1). In a bantering dialogue between Katharina and Petruchio, Petruchio declares that he would play cock to Katharina's hen. She retorts: 'No cock of mine, you crow too like a *craven*.' Lord Campbell jumped to the conclusion that this was a reference to the cry of 'Craven' by a defeated combatant in a

Trial by Battle. But, as is made clear by the context, Katharina's reference is not to 'wager of battle' but to cock-fighting. In sporting parlance, a cock that was not game was called a 'craven'. This is one of several instances in which Lord Campbell was mistaken in supposing that he had discovered a legal allusion in the plays.

BENEFIT OF CLERGY

Benefit of Clergy was an extraordinary privilege enjoyed by literate folk in Shakespeare's day. A 'clerk', or in other words a person who could read, if convicted of any of a certain class of crimes, was enabled to claim exemption from the punishment of death. Besides receiving a substituted punishment, he was branded in the thumb and was disabled from claiming the privilege a second time. Accordingly we find Jack Cade reproaching Lord Say with having put poor men in prison, 'and because they could not read, thou hast hanged them'. In another place in the same play, Dick the Butcher drops a significant aside. When Jack Cade said, 'I fear neither sword nor fire,' Dick remarks, 'But, methinks, he should stand in fear of fire, being burnt i' the hand for stealing of sheep' (2 *Henry VI*, iv. 2 and 7).

CRIMINAL LAW

A DISCHARGED PRISONER'S FEE

According to an ancient custom, to which allusion is twice made in the plays, a prisoner, even when he was innocent, had to pay a fee to his jailer on being discharged from custody. Traces of this notorious anomaly continued to linger in our prison procedure until a comparatively recent date. At least five of Shakespeare's contemporaries referred to it; and Shakespeare alluded to it twice. In the Third Part of *King Henry VI* (iv. 6) the King, in the expectation of his liberation from imprisonment, inquires from the Lieutenant of the Tower, 'At our enlargement what are thy due fees?' In *Winter's Tale* (i. 2) Hermione is dissuading Polixenes from leaving Sicily. She asks whether, by refusing to remain her guest, he will force her to keep him as a prisoner 'so you shall pay your fees, when you depart, and save your thanks'.

ALLUSIONS TO CROWN, CRIMINAL, CONSTITUTIONAL AND FEUDAL LAW
(CONTINUED)

CHAPTER X

ALLUSIONS TO CROWN, CRIMINAL, CONSTITUTIONAL AND FEUDAL LAW
(CONTINUED)

PUNISHMENTS AND TORTURE

PUNISHMENTS, in Tudor and Jacobean times, were swift and terrible. Most terrible of all was the punishment meted out to traitors, who were publicly hanged, drawn and quartered. Shakespeare, in *King John* (ii. 2), makes Philip the Bastard speak of the Dauphin as 'love's traitor', receiving a traitor's punishment at Blanche's hands. He is described as '*drawn* in the flattering table of her eye!—*hang'd* in the frowning wrinkle of her brow!—and *quarter'd* in her heart'.

Burning was referred to by Shakespeare as the punishment both of witchcraft and of heresy. In the Second Part of *King Henry VI* (ii. 3) the King orders a witch in Smithfield to be 'burn'd to ashes'; in *King Lear* (iii. 2) the fool foretells the downfall of England, when there are 'no hereticks burn'd'. In *Romeo and Juliet* (i. 2) the burning of heretics is turned to poetical account. Benvolio says that he could show Romeo faces in Verona so superior to Juliet's that they will make him 'think his swan a crow'. Romeo replies indignantly that, if he should ever tell such a falsehood, his tears would turn to fires, and his eyes 'transparent hereticks be burnt for liars!'

The infliction of torture is mentioned in the Second Part of *King Henry VI* (iii. 3); and Shakespeare frequently used the idea of torture to express mental suffering, or to describe the pains of hell and purgatory in the next world. He was disposed to make light of the stocks and of the pillory. One of Shakespeare's funniest speeches is Launce's colloquy with his dog Crab in the *Two Gentlemen of Verona* (iv. 4). Launce indulges in reminiscences of the many indignities which he had suffered on account of Crab's misdeeds. He relates (among other incidents) how he had 'sat in the stocks' for the puddings his dog Crab had stolen, and how he had 'stood on the pillory' for the geese that Crab had killed. When Katharina in the *Taming of the Shrew* (ii. 1) breaks a lute over Hortensio's

CRIMINAL LAW

head, Hortensio describes himself as standing amazed looking through the lute 'as on a pillory'. The Lord Chief Justice's threat to punish Falstaff 'by the heels' (2 *Henry IV*, i. 2) covered an allusion to putting persons in irons or in the stocks. This phrase, like a similar one 'in handfast' (*Winter's Tale*, iv. 3), which Shakespeare uses, had become quite non-technical. We also have references, here and there, to whippings, fines and imprisonments, as well as to those grim officers of justice the 'common executioner' and the 'common hangman'.

PREROGATIVE AND PRIZE LAW

Shakespeare refers to certain exercises of the royal prerogative, such as the impressment of soldiers and seamen and the purveyance of horses for the public service, which were notoriously abused by the King's officers from Plantagenet times down to the reign of James I. Nobody who knows anything about Sir John Falstaff will be surprised at the frank confession which he makes of his evil doings as an officer in King Henry IV's army: 'I have misused the King's press damnably,' he says (iv. 2). It appears that he had released one hundred and fifty capable recruits in exchange for bribes amounting to three hundred and odd pounds. On the other hand, he had mercilessly impressed all those who could not pay. They consisted of 'a hundred and fifty tattered prodigals' and 'scarecrows'; and they presented such a forlorn appearance that a passer-by remarked that Sir John must have 'unloaded all the gibbets and pressed the dead bodies' into the King's service. The fat knight was equally unscrupulous in exercising the right of 'purveyance'. 'Let us take any man's horses,' he exclaimed, 'the laws of England are at my commandment' (2 *Henry IV*, v. 3). Sir John Falstaff is found insisting upon another military privilege. He claimed to have been advised by 'learned counsel in the laws' that while engaged upon active service he was not bound to obey a summons to appear before the Courts (2 *Henry IV*, i. 2).

In the Third Part of *King Henry VI* (ii. 5), we see the operation of the system of impressment in the War of the Roses. The dramatist tells us what befell a father and son. The father was 'press'd' by the Yorkist Earl of Warwick to fight for the White Rose, while the son was 'pressed' by the King to fight for the Red Rose of Lancaster. In *Hamlet* (i. 1) Marcellus inquires the reason of the warlike preparations which are afoot in Denmark. One of his questions: 'Why such impress of shipwrights?' has been referred

CONSTITUTIONAL LAW

to in our Law Courts in comparatively recent times to illustrate the extent to which the right of impressment was formerly carried. Achilles, in *Troilus and Cressida* (ii. 1), taunts Thersites with having soldiered 'under an impress' instead of as a volunteer.

'Lawful Prize' depended on the law of war rather than upon the prerogative of the Crown. It was a familiar idea in Shakespeare's time, and frequently cropped up in the dramas of that day. Shakespeare introduces it figuratively in *Othello* (i. 2), when Iago refers to Othello's carrying off of Desdemona as the 'boarding of a land carack' (i.e. galleon), and he adds: 'If it prove lawful prize, he's made for ever.' Again, in *King Richard III* (iii. 7), Buckingham, referring to Elizabeth Woodville's success in captivating King Edward IV, says that she 'made prize and purchase of his wanton eye'.

CONSTITUTIONAL LAW

When Shakespeare alluded to points of Constitutional Law, he usually borrowed them from the Chronicles which were the sources of his historical plays. It was from the Chronicles that he learned all about the doctrine of the Supremacy of the Crown, which was so much in evidence in Tudor times, and about the

Constitutional principle that the Judges, when acting in their judicial capacity, were the deputies of the King. He makes Chief Justice Gascoigne explain the principle when justifying himself to King Henry V for having committed him to prison for contempt of court when he had been Prince of Wales. He represents Gascoigne as expounding the doctrine to the King on his accession: 'I then did use the person of your father; the image of his power lay then in me.'

The dramatist also gleaned from the Chronicles the true nature of the office of Lord Chancellor, who was appointed by the delivery to him of the Great Seal, and was discharged from office either by the voluntary surrender of the Great Seal into the hands of the Sovereign, or by the Sovereign demanding it in person or sending a messenger for it under the sign-manual. In *King Richard III* (ii. 4) the Archbishop of York offered to act irregularly when he suggested to the widow of King Edward IV, 'I'll resign unto your grace the seal I keep.' Wolsey understood his office better. When the Dukes of Suffolk and Norfolk demanded the Great Seal from the fallen Cardinal, he insisted upon receiving a command from the King under the sign-manual (*Henry VIII*, iii. 2).

HENRY WRIOTHESLEY, 3RD EARL OF SOUTHAMPTON

A MEMBER OF GRAY'S INN
SHAKESPEARE'S PATRON

(*Pages* xxxv, 26, 28, 30, 32, 107)

FEUDAL LAW

VASSALAGE AND VILLEINAGE

A vassal was a tenant or feudatory who held of a superior lord. Shakespeare, in a sonnet which probably was addressed to Southampton, hails him as 'lord of my love', and describes himself as being 'in vassalage' to his patron's merit. Elsewhere he associated vassalage with the idea of subjection or inferiority. When Cæsar notices a withered look in Pompey's countenance since last they met, Pompey replies that harsh fortune may work changes in his face —'But in my bosom shall she never come, to make my heart a vassal' (*Antony and Cleopatra*, ii. 6). When Troilus (*Troilus and Cressida*, iii. 3) displays agitation and nervousness at the approach of Cressida, he compares himself to a 'vassal' who unawares encounters 'the eye of Majesty'.

The villeins were the bondmen or slaves of the feudal system, and were bound to their lords by an oath of fealty more servile than that of freeholders. In Elizabeth's time villeinage was gradually disappearing as the result partly of economic causes and partly of the practice of manumission or enfranchisement. In the *Two Gentlemen of Verona* (ii. 4) Valentine playfully refers to Proteus's eyes as Sylvia's faithless bondmen. He says: 'Belike, that now she hath enfranchised them upon some other pawn for fealty'; and receives the reply: 'Nay, sure, I think she holds them prisoners still.'

ALLUSIONS TO THE LAW OF REAL PROPERTY

CHAPTER XI
ALLUSIONS TO THE LAW OF REAL PROPERTY[1]

THERE was no branch of the law with which Shakespeare had better opportunities of becoming acquainted than the law of Real Property. Following in the footsteps of his father, he invested his earnings in the purchase of real estate both in Stratford and in London. He also became a mortgagor and a lessee of lands and acquired an interest in common lands in the neighbourhood of Stratford. These experiences were sufficient to account for most of the knowledge of which his plays afford evidence.

FEE SIMPLE, FEE FARM, SALE AND MORTGAGE

Shakespeare, being aware that to 'stand seized' (*Hamlet*, i. 1) 'in fee simple' was to enjoy the highest possible estate in land, sometimes used

[1] For other allusions to the Law of Real Property see Chapter VII.

the words 'fee simple' to express totality or absoluteness. The devil is referred to as having an estate 'in fee-simple with fine and recovery' in Sir John Falstaff (*Merry Wives of Windsor*, iv. 2). Parolles describes the reckless Captain Dumain as one who 'for a *quart d'ecu* will sell the fee-simple of his salvation' (*All's Well That Ends Well*, iv. 3). He paints a quarrelsome daredevil as a person 'the fee-simple' of whose life 'any man should buy for an hour and a quarter' (*Romeo and Juliet*, iii. 1). He compares a long embrace to an estate for ever at a fee farm rent, for he makes Pandarus invite Troilus and Cressida to indulge in 'a kiss in fee-farm' (*Troilus and Cressida*, iii. 2).

Hamlet's speech in the churchyard scene (v. 1), when he picks up what he supposes to be a lawyer's skull, contains a long string of conveyancing tags which will be noticed in another chapter. Elsewhere we find evidence that the poet knew that land could be 'bargain'd for and sold' (2 *Henry VI*, i. 1), or 'sold in fee' (*Hamlet*, iv. 4), or that a purchaser could be 'enfeoffed' of it. The weak and vain King Richard II is described as having 'enfeoff'd himself to popularity' (1 *Henry IV*, iii. 2).

In the 134th Sonnet the poet tells us that he has mortgaged himself to a friend, and, as a

THE LAW OF REAL PROPERTY

collateral security, has executed a bond with a surety. He forfeits his estate to the mortgagee, and his surety is sued for the debt. He finds himself in default to both friend and surety. 'He pays the whole, and yet am I not free.' In *As You Like It* (iii. 1) we have a reference to the writ of 'extent', which was the common writ of execution against the lands of a judgment debtor.

LANDLORD AND TENANT

A lease was a conception which had a fascination for Shakespeare. Such ideas as the transcience of beauty, of happiness, of human effort, and of human life suggested to his imagination an analogy to what he once described as 'leases of short-numbered hours'. Life was for him 'a lease of nature' (*Macbeth*, iv. 1). Beauty was a fugitive estate which was 'held in lease'.

When he is promising to make a friend immortal by his verse, he tells him that 'summer's lease hath all too short a date', and confidently adds: 'But thy eternal summer shall not fade.' When he exhorts a friend to marry and to carry on in his children his 'sweet form' and 'semblance', he reinforces his advice by the argument, 'So should that beauty which you hold in lease find no determination.' The

146th Sonnet is founded upon the idea that the immortal soul is the tenant of a perishable tenement. One couplet will serve as a specimen: 'Why so large cost, having so short a lease, Dost thou upon thy fading mansion spend?' Elsewhere we find Valentine speaking of his heart as 'tenantless' when Sylvia leaves him (*Two Gentlemen of Verona*, v. 4), Horatio telling how a little before Cæsar's death the Roman graves stood 'tenantless' and 'the sheeted dead did squeak and gibber in the Roman streets' (*Hamlet*, i. 1), and the gravediggers (v. 1) coming to the conclusion that no building is more durable than a gallows because it 'outlives a thousand tenants'.

COMMONS

A 'common of pasture', in its most technical sense, meant a *right* of pasture exercisable by one or more persons over another person's lands. Shakespeare used the word in a less technical sense. He applied it to the *lands* over which such rights were exercisable. For example, Antony, in *Julius Cæsar* (iv. 1), suggests to Octavius to rid themselves of their colleague Lepidus by turning him off 'like to the empty ass, to shake his ears, and graze in commons'. In the *Comedy of Errors* (ii. 2), when Antipholus of Syracuse rebukes his servant for wast-

THE LAW OF REAL PROPERTY

ing his master's valuable time by his unseasonable jests, he complains that 'your sauciness' will 'make a common of my serious hours'.

In Queen Elizabeth's time the Courts were often occupied with the disputes which arose between the commoners *inter se*. A frequent cause of complaint among the commoners was the overcharging of the common by one or more of them with a larger number of sheep or cattle than the proper quota. This is alluded to in the *Two Gentlemen of Verona* (i. 1), where Proteus and Speed are discussing 'sheep' under the name of 'muttons'. Speed introduces such a superfluity of 'muttons' into his conversation that Proteus says banteringly that 'Here's too small a pasture for such a store of muttons.' Speed replies that 'if the ground be overcharged' Proteus will have his remedy.

A burning question in Medieval England was the inclosure of common lands by the owners of the soil. It was a frequent subject of litigation, of agitation, and of legislation. Parliament began to control the power of inclosure by the Statute of Merton in 1235; and, before the controversy was settled by the Inclosure Act of 1845, more than four thousand Acts of Parliament, public or private, regulating the subject of the inclosure of commons were placed upon the Statute Book. The conflict between the overlords and the commoners about the inclosure of commons was acute in Shakespeare's day, and was particularly so in Stratford-on-Avon.

The notoriety of this public question is reflected in the Second Part of *King Henry VI* (i. 3), of which play Shakespeare was part author. The Duke of Suffolk figures as the harsh overlord of 'the commons of Melford'. A commoner comes to the Royal Palace in order to protest against the inclosure of the commons. He is described as 'a poor petitioner of our whole township'; and he is so unlucky as to hand his petition to the Duke himself, who calls him a 'knave' and dismisses him summarily. In the same play we find that one of the principal planks in Jack Cade's communistic programme was the abolition of all exclusive rights of property in pasture lands—'All the realm', shouted Cade, 'shall be in common, and in Cheapside shall my palfrey go to grass' (2 *Henry VI*, iv. 2).

COMMON AND SEVERAL

The word *several* as opposed to *common* has had various uses in our Law. One of its meanings, in Shakespeare's time, was to describe land

THE LAW OF REAL PROPERTY

privately or separately owned or occupied, of which a good example was a plot of pastureland which had been inclosed or allotted to an individual. This meaning has become obsolete except in a few localities. But it was so well known as to have passed into general use in the fifteenth, sixteenth and seventeenth centuries. The standard dictionaries (e.g. the Oxford Dict., A 7; C 1 and 2) contain numerous instances of its use in this sense by writers who were not lawyers. Among them were Ben Jonson, George Chapman and Thomas Fuller. Accordingly there is no cause for surprise when we find Shakespeare, in the 137th Sonnet, moralizing upon the blindness of Love, and asking himself why he should think that to be 'a several plot' which his heart knew to be the wide world's 'common place'?

A similar distinction between 'common' and 'several' is alluded to loosely in *Love's Labour's Lost* (ii. 1). A courtier and a Maid of Honour are indulging in a duel of pun and persiflage about 'sheep' and 'pasture'. The courtier requests the lady to 'grant him pasture', which was his way of asking for leave to kiss her. She replies, 'Not so, gentle beast, my lips are no common, though several they be.' Here we have a reference to the well-known contrast between 'common' and 'several'. There is also, perhaps, a play upon another meaning of the word 'several' which, as applied to the lips, might mean 'separate from each other'. Such a pun would explain the use of the preposition 'though', which, if the poet wished to express nothing more than a contrast between 'common' and 'several', would be out of place. It has been pointed out that there must be some underlying subtlety to explain the conjunctive word 'though'.

Some commentators have supposed that in this passage the poet was referring to the more technical conception of a *right* of common. But the lady's lips are not being compared to a *right*, but to a *place*.

William Shakespeare became personally involved in a dispute over an inclosure of common lands in and about Stratford-on-Avon. The overlords were his fellow-townsmen Thomas and William Combe. He refrained from taking sides in the controversy, contenting himself with protecting his own interests by coming to terms with the brothers Combe. The experience of the commoners of Stratford in this respect was not exceptional. The inclosure of commons presented as familiar a problem to the Elizabethans as the conflict between Capital and Labour does in our time.

SHAKESPEARE'S USE OF
LEGAL MAXIMS

CHAPTER XII
SHAKESPEARE'S USE OF LEGAL MAXIMS

THE introduction into their plays of legal maxims was a common practice of the Elizabethan playwrights In his method of using them Shakespeare differed characteristically from his fellows. Other dramatists are found introducing them in the original Latin or in their translated English form. Shakespeare very seldom did so. When he made use of them, it was in some assimilated or applied form. For example, the Latin maxim '*Dormiunt aliquando leges, moriuntur nunquam*' seems to find an echo in Angelo's words in *Measure for Measure* (ii. 2), 'the law hath not been dead, though it hath slept.' Shakespeare seems to have stolen the thought without its Latin drapery, leaving us in doubt whether the idea was borrowed from the maxim, or was an original flash from his own creative mind.

SHAKESPEARE AND THE LAW

ÆDIFICIUM SOLO CEDIT

A typical example of the difference between Shakespeare's methods and those of his contemporaries was afforded by their respective use of a Latin maxim which was to the effect that, if a man by mistake erected a house with his own materials upon another man's land, the house became the property of the owner of the soil. So serious a result of an innocent mistake surprised the public and was taken up by the dramatists. One of them, George Chapman, who was not a lawyer, actually quoted the Latin maxim in an abbreviated form, '*Ædificium solo cedit*'. Shakespeare, on the other hand, without mentioning the maxim or making any display of legal technicality, weaved the idea into an ordinary piece of dialogue. In the *Merry Wives of Windsor* (ii. 2) one of the characters is trying to induce Falstaff to aid him in a love intrigue, in which he has spent time and money without reaping any success. Falstaff asks him of what quality was his love. He replies: 'Like a fair house, built upon another man's ground; so that I have lost my edifice, by mistaking the place where I erected it.' The advocates of the theory that Shakespeare must have been a lawyer lay great stress upon this passage. It might almost be described as their *pièce de résistance*.

MR. RUSHTON'S 'SHAKESPEARE'S LEGAL MAXIMS'

A great deal of misplaced ingenuity has been directed to the discovery of legal maxims in the Shakespearian plays. For example, a learned little book by Mr. W. L. Rushton, entitled *Shakespeare's Legal Maxims*, was calculated to create an erroneous impression. The author cited some forty maxims of the law which he connected with passages in Shakespeare's plays. A competent critic has hit off the book very happily when he described it as 'a painstaking performance' with an element of 'laborious trifling' about it. The author seems, in the great majority of his instances, to have allowed himself to be misled by some superficial similarity. The remotest semblance of analogy between a legal maxim and a passage in Shakespeare's plays was calculated to lead him astray upon a false scent.

EXAMPLES OF MISPLACED INGENUITY

For example, Shakespeare sometimes refers poetically to such elementary principles of Justice as that crime should not go unpunished, that impunity encourages criminality, or that justice should not be arbitrary or partial. Tragedy and Melodrama, without the help of impressive generalities such as these, would be poor indeed. But Mr. Rushton treated these literary commonplaces as if they were technical aphorisms of juristic science. He produced passages from ancient law-books which were to the same effect, and he would have us believe that the dramatist picked his diamonds out of these dustbins.

PEDANTICAL ANALOGIES

Troilus, when Hector belittles Cressida, defends himself and his infatuation for the lady by asking Hector 'what is aught, but as 'tis valued?' (*Troilus and Cressida*, ii. 2). Mr. Rushton drags in an irrelevant axiom of Coke's, that 'things are worth as much as they will sell for'. When Richard II (iv. 1), finding that no man will respond 'Amen' to his 'God Save the King', asks despairingly, 'Am I both priest and clerk?' Rushton cites a totally irrelevant maxim about the relation to each other of kings and clerics. When Lady Macbeth (ii. 2), in discussing the psychology of murder, contrasts the 'attempt' and the 'deed', Rushton supposes Shakespeare to have borrowed this simple thought from a

LEGAL MAXIMS

ponderous passage in the Institutes about the difference between *conatus* and *effectus*.

When Hamlet (iv. 3) says to the King that 'man and wife is one flesh', Mr. Rushton supposes that Shakespeare was thinking of the maxim that 'man and wife are regarded as one person (*quasi unica persona*)', which means that during marriage the wife's legal existence is regarded by the Common Law as merged in that of her husband. But surely the poet was thinking of a simpler and loftier idea about the closeness of the marriage tie, which was expressed in Christ's saying that 'man and wife shall be no more twain but one flesh'.

Again, when the conceptions 'Possession' and 'Right' are opposed to each other in a dialogue in *King John* (i. 1), Mr. Rushton (followed by Lord Campbell) supposes the dramatist to be making use of the maxim,'*In aequali jure melior est conditio possidentis*'. But the maxim does not represent the idea of the Shakespearian passage, in which the ideas of right and possession are contrasted, but without any suggestion that, where rights are equal, there is a presumption or advantage on the side of possession. Again, Mr. Rushton finds in the simple reflection that 'a passed sentence cannot be recalled' a reference to the maxim, '*sententia interlocutoria revocari potest definitiva non potest*'. But the point of the maxim (namely, the difference in the effect of an *interlocutory* and a *final* order) is altogether absent from the Shakespearian line.

When a dying soldier, in *King John* (v. 4), supports the truth of what he says by reminding his hearers that he is at the point of death, Rushton seems to suppose that Shakespeare was thinking about the rules of the Law of Evidence about 'dying declarations'. When Diana, in *All's Well That Ends Well* (iv. 2), refers to the solemnity of an oath whereby we 'take the Highest to witness', Rushton supposes that she was consciously expounding the Latin maxim '*jurare est deum in testem vocare*'. When Antony (*Antony and Cleopatra*, i. 3) pleads 'the strong necessity of time' (or in other words 'another pressing engagement') for leaving Cleopatra, Rushton supposes the poet to have in mind the maxim '*necessitas est lex temporis*', which sounds like what Antony said, but embodies a totally different idea.

Of a similar description are more than thirty out of the forty maxims which this enthusiastic searcher for legal flotsam and jetsam has detected in Shakespeare, as if his plays had been metrical versions of the Year Books. It is doubtful whether there are half a dozen real references

LEGAL MAXIMS

to the maxims of the law in the whole range of the thirty-seven Shakespearian plays. Two of them were cited at the commencement of this chapter. There is a passage in *King Henry VIII* (v. 2) which looks like an allusion to the principle that it is the function of a judge to decide questions of law and of a jury to decide questions of fact. Then there is Phœbe's remark in *As You Like It* (iii. 5) that 'omittance is no quittance'. But here we have a maxim which had become proverbial. There are plenty of proverbs to be found in Shakespeare's plays, but he very seldom introduced legal maxims into his dialogues.

SHAKESPEARE'S USE OF
LEGAL JARGON

K

CHAPTER XIII
SHAKESPEARE'S USE OF LEGAL JARGON

ONE of the characteristic traits of the Elizabethan drama was the use of legal jargon, both in poetical passages and in comic scenes. For example, written instruments under seal (which were referred to as 'deeds' or 'indentures' or 'specialties') were so commonly used as symbols of love and kisses by poets of that day that the metaphor would have become trite, if Shakespeare had not made it immortal in such passages as 'But my kisses bring again, seals of love, but seal'd in vain' (*Measure for Measure*, iv. 1), and in Venus's invitation to Adonis to 'Set thy seal-manual on my wax-red lips' (*Venus and Adonis*, 516) Jack Cade treated seals and wax in a humorous vein. 'Is not this a lamentable thing', said he, 'that of the skin of an innocent lamb should be made parchment? That parchment, being scribbled o'er, should undo a man?

Some say, the bee stings; but I say it is the bee's wax, for I did but seal once a thing, and I was never mine own man since' (2 *Henry VI*, iv. 2).

Shakespeare, like other poets, turned 'bonds', 'mortgages' and 'charters' to poetic use. He tells of bonds of 'love', of 'fellowship', of 'board and bed', of 'fate', and of 'heaven'. Sometimes the word 'bond' means the strict minimum of duty, as when Cordelia alienates her father's favour by saying 'I love your majesty according to my bond; nor more nor less' (*Lear*, i. 1). To a friend the poet describes himself as 'mortgaged to thy will'. A 'charter' for him spelt liberty. Jaques tells the banished Duke, 'I must have liberty withal, as large a charter as the wind, to blow on whom I please' (*As You Like It*, ii. 7). In the same sense we find, in *King Henry V* (i. 1), the air spoken of as 'a charter'd libertine'; and in *Othello* (i. 3) Desdemona appealing to the Duke of Venice to 'let me find a charter in your voice'.

In *As You Like It* (ii. 1) the legal conceptions of 'bankruptcy' and of a 'will' (in the sense of a testamentary instrument) are applied to the pitiable situation of a wounded deer. Jaques, observing a wounded deer being treated with indifference by its comrades, thus addressed the

LEGAL JARGON

careless herd: 'Sweep on, you fat and greasy citizens, 'Tis just the fashion: wherefore do you look upon that poor and broken bankrupt there?' The creature's tears as they fall into a passing stream made him think of the testament 'of a worldling' who 'gives more to that which had too much'.

'Pawn' frequently occurs as a word of reproach. For example, it is thrice applied to King Richard III. Buckingham, complaining of Richard's broken promise, reproaches him with having 'pawn'd his honour and his faith'. King Edward IV's widowed Queen reproaches him with having blemished his Garter, and with having 'pawn'd his knightly virtue' (*Richard III*, iv. 2 and 4). The word 'earnest' is used to express a part payment as pledge or security for the whole, or more frequently as a token of something more to come hereafter. In the latter sense Macbeth was made Thane of Cawdor 'for earnest of a greater honour' (*Macbeth*, i. 3).

LEGAL PHRASES AND TAGS

Scattered through the plays are tags, which were the hackneyed embroideries of deeds, agreements, indictments or other conventional documents. Such are 'sealed interchangeably', 'contrary to the faith and allegiance of a true subject', 'contrary to the King, his crown and dignity', 'immediately provided in that case', 'words such as no Christian can endure', or 'free as heart can wish or tongue can tell'; and we find a parody of legal tautology in the words 'which here thou viewest, beholdest, surveyest, or seest' in *Love's Labour's Lost* (i. 1).

Latin law phrases were used freely by Shakespeare's contemporaries. Ben Jonson gives us twenty of them in one page. Shakespeare with his 'little Latin and less Greek' was as sparing in their use as he was in the use of Latin maxims. Those which he occasionally indulged in were of a very trivial description, such as *suum cuique, cum privilegio ad imprimendum, se offendendo* (a play on *se defendendo*), *absque hoc*, which was the commencement of almost every traverse in the old system of special pleading, and *imprimis*. Latin quotations of this kind were no more recondite than old Mr. Weller's regretful allusion to an *alibi* was in Charles Dickens's day.

Hamlet's speech over the lawyer's skull is a legal storehouse. He begins by asking 'where be his quiddits now, his quillets, his cases, his tenures, and his tricks?' Then he branches off into the jargon of the conveyancers: 'This fellow might be in's time a great buyer of

LEGAL JARGON

land, with his statutes, his recognizances, his fines, his double vouchers, his recoveries.' A mere catalogue of this kind does not necessarily denote any technical knowledge. This string of tags sounds archaic in the twentieth century. In the sixteenth century they were modern, and were likely to win a laugh from an audience which comprised a strong legal element.

LEGAL PUNS

Several of Shakespeare's legal puns have been mentioned in previous chapters.[1] There are plenty of others. In *As You Like It* (i. 2), when Le Beau describes the wrestlers as 'three proper young men of excellent growth and *presence*', Rosalind replies, 'With bills on their necks,—"Be it known unto all men *by these presents*".' These were the opening words of almost every deed poll, and must have been well known to theatre-goers, because we find other dramatists alluding to them, and giving them in their Latin form, *'noverint universi'*.

In *Romeo and Juliet* (i. 3) there occurs a supposed pun upon the word 'cover.' When Lady Capulet recommends Paris to Juliet, she compares him to an unbound book, and says, 'To beautify him, only lacks a cover.' Here there

[1] *Vide* pp. 74 and 117.

is possibly a play on the word 'cover', which signifies both the 'cover' of a book, and the condition of a married woman or a 'feme covert'. The occurrence of a legal pun in this place is not so clear as in our other examples.

Dogberry gives us a play on the word 'steal' when he instructs the Constable of the Watch that 'the most peaceable way for you, if you do take a thief, is, to let him show himself what he is, and *steal out* of your company' (*Much Ado About Nothing*, iii. 3). In a more serious context the same pun occurs in *All's Well That Ends Well* (iii. 2), where Helena announces her approaching flight in the words 'Come, night, end, day! For, with the dark, poor thief, I'll *steal* away.'

A complex pun upon the words 'manner' and 'form' occurs in *Love's Labour's Lost* (i. 1). When a thief was caught *flagrante delicto* he was said to be 'taken with the manner', which was a corruption of an Anglo-Norman phrase 'with the mainor', i.e. with the thing stolen in his hand. More than a century before Shakespeare began to write plays this phrase had passed into current use as a synonym for 'caught in the act'. Costard uses it in *Love's Labour's Lost* when he is making a frank disclosure to Biron of the details of his flirtation with a country wench

LEGAL JARGON

named Jaquenetta. Biron asks him 'In what *manner*?' Costard replies: 'In *manner* and *form* following, sir . . . I was seen with her in the *manor*-house, sitting with her upon the *form*.'

Legal puns were in the fashion upon the stage in Shakespeare's day. For example, we find another dramatist punning on the words '*counterpart*' and 'counterpane'.

LORD CAMPBELL'S EXAGGERATION OF SHAKESPEARE'S LEGAL ACQUIREMENTS

CHAPTER XIV
LORD CAMPBELL'S EXAGGERATION OF SHAKESPEARE'S LEGAL ACQUIREMENTS

A MODERN CONTROVERSY

MORE than a hundred and seventy years elapsed after Shakespeare's death before anybody showed surprise at his legal allusiveness. Nobody would have been surprised, if the works of the other Elizabethan dramatists had been better known. But, while the Shakespearian plays had grown in popularity, those of his contemporaries had passed into a comparative oblivion. As a result, some of the critics of the latter part of the eighteenth century mistook Shakespeare for a forensic phenomenon, when he had only been a type of a forensic fashion. His legalisms were not more numerous and were less technical than those of the other poets and dramatists. Where he surpassed the others was in his superior grace and ease in handling legal phrases, which, as Mr. Grant White happily expressed it, 'flowed from his pen as part of his vocabulary, and as parcel of his thoughts'.

WAS SHAKESPEARE AN ATTORNEY'S CLERK?

The first commentator to express surprise at Shakespeare's legal erudition was Edmund Malone, a non-practising lawyer, who attained real distinction as a Shakespearian critic. He naïvely admitted that he had to brush up his 'black-letter law' in order to understand what Shakespeare was alluding to. Failing to realize that what he called 'black-letter' had not been so 'black' in the sixteenth century, he hazarded a suggestion that the dramatist might have been a clerk in an attorney's office at Stratford. The suggestion received scant attention until seventy years afterwards, when Mr. Payne Collier succeeded in inducing Lord Campbell to take up the subject and to write a brochure entitled *Shakespeare's Legal Acquirements*.

LORD CAMPBELL'S BROCHURE

Lord Campbell did not say that Shakespeare must have been trained to the Law. But the gist of his argument is that he probably was so. It is needless to say that, from a legal point of view, his brochure was extremely well furnished. But when Lord Campbell took up

SOME EXAGGERATIONS

Elizabethan literature, he appears to have undertaken to explore an unfamiliar continent. In his voyage of discovery he collected some weird legalisms, and discerned law-points which were not visible to the ordinary eye. He also lit up the subject with some sparkling comments. For example, he wrote that 'to Shakespeare's law, lavishly as he propounds it, there can neither be demurrer nor bill of exceptions, nor writ of error'. These remedies are obviously inapplicable to a poet's quips and metaphors; and this sentence, which is characteristic of Lord Campbell and has been quoted *ad nauseam*, savours of a rhetorical truism.

A WORTHLESS PIECE OF EXTERNAL
EVIDENCE

Lord Campbell's only piece of external evidence was Thomas Nashe's allusion to an 'English Seneca' who had left 'the trade of Noverint' (i.e. of law-scrivener) 'and was capable of writing whole Hamlets'. It is now agreed that this allusion was not to Shakespeare, but to Kyd, a tragedian, son and assistant of a law-scrivener, who was author of an early Hamlet which was one of the sources of Shakespeare's masterpiece. When this piece of external evidence had been disposed of, nothing

SHAKESPEARE AND THE LAW

remained to support Lord Campbell's argument except the *pot-pourri* of legal scraps which he collected from the plays and poems.

LORD CAMPBELL'S EVIDENCE FROM THE HISTORICAL PLAYS

The King, in the opening scene of *King John*, decides that Philip Faulconbridge, who was notoriously the issue of an adulterous amour, was a legitimate Faulconbridge because he was born in wedlock. Lord Campbell treats the King's decision as evidence that Shakespeare 'uniformly lays down good law', and describes it as a 'sound' and 'perspicuous' application of the maxim '*Pater est quem nuptiæ demonstrant*'. But the incident was taken from the old play of 'The Troublesome Raigne of King John'. It merely illustrates the dramatist's happy knack of burnishing rusty materials.

Lord Campbell made much of Shakespeare's reference (1 *Henry IV*, iii. 1) to the 'indentures tripartite' by which Mortimer Glendower and Hotspur proposed to divide England, and he suggested that it was a reminiscence of the poet's early days as an attorney's clerk. But the whole incident, including the word 'tripartite', comes from the Chronicles; and the phrase 'indentures tripartite' cannot have been

[144]

THE COURT OF WARDS
PRESIDED OVER BY LORD BURLEIGH

(*Pages* 26, 150)

SOME EXAGGERATIONS

very recondite, since it occurs in one of Ben Jonson's brightest comedies.

In the same play Lord Campbell supposed that he had found a significant law term, where King Henry IV pretends that he had come to England to 'sue his livery', i.e. to obtain delivery of his lands from the Court of Wards upon his coming of age. But the incident was derived from an historical source; and the 'law term' was in such common use that we find the poet Donne, when he wished to express the idea of the God of Love reaching years of discretion, borrowing the phrase and writing that 'our little Cupid hath sued his livery and is no more in minority.'

As evidence of the dramatist's 'deep technical knowledge of law', Lord Campbell cited a reference to the 'omnivorous' nature of the writ of præmunire (*Henry VIII*, iii. 2) under which Cardinal Wolsey was to forfeit all his 'goods, lands, tenements, chattels, and whatsoever, and to be out of the King's protection.' These words (save for a slight transposition in order to turn prose into verse) were taken verbatim from the Chronicles, and afforded evidence of nothing except that the author, when it suited him, could be an accurate copyist.

Shakespeare's references to the constitutional doctrine of the Supremacy of the Crown, to

Queen Katherine's Challenge of Wolsey as her judge, and to Wolsey's refusal to surrender the Great Seal without receiving the King's command by letters patent, have been bandied about by Lord Campbell and others in the controversy about Shakespeare's legal knowledge, although these incidents were derived by the poet from historical and not from legal sources.

'ROMEO AND JULIET'

The opening scenes of *Romeo and Juliet* turn upon a feud between the houses of Montague and Capulet, which was causing 'civil strife' in 'fair Verona'. When a Capulet advises his clan to keep cool and to content themselves with frowning and biting their thumbs at the Montagues, Lord Campbell detects an allusion to the technicalities of the law of Assault, and seriously suggests that the Capulet wished to provoke an assault so as to lead up to a plea of self-defence. When the Prince threatens the brawlers that their 'lives shall pay the forfeit of the peace', Lord Campbell suggests that they were 'being bound over in the English fashion to keep the peace'.

'THE MERCHANT OF VENICE'

Lord Campbell puzzles his readers when he writes that the trial in the *Merchant of Venice*

SOME EXAGGERATIONS

was 'duly conducted according to the strict rules of legal procedure'. The procedure from our English standpoint looks strange and unfamiliar. The Duke presides, but does not adjudicate. He remits the cause to a jurisconsult of Padua, who sends a young doctor of Rome to the Court as his deputy. The young doctor disposes of the case without hearing oral evidence. This way of trying a case by referring it to a Doctor of Laws came from the Italian original. Some such procedure was prevalent in medieval Spain and Italy. Modern travellers have met with examples of a similar procedure in Mexico and Nicaragua, where the Hispano-Americans seem to have preserved it like a 'fly in amber'. Several other fanciful legalisms have been discovered in the same play. For example, when a Venetian jailer is reproached by Shylock for 'coming abroad' with his prisoner, Lord Campbell detects a law point, and hazards the suggestion that the Jew is threatening to bring a common law action of 'Escape' against the jailer.

'KING LEAR'

King Lear (iii. 6) orders his unnatural daughters to be arraigned before a tribunal composed of the 'deranged' Edgar and the Court Fool who is described as Edgar's 'Yokefellow of Equity'. One of the members of this ill-assorted criminal tribunal opens the proceedings by singing two comic songs. The King acts as prosecutor, and then gives judgment without consulting the judges. Lord Campbell puzzles us by claiming that the trial is 'conducted in a manner showing a perfect familiarity with legal procedure'. It seems even more extravagant than the procedure with which W. S. Gilbert made us familiar.

'OTHELLO'

Lord Campbell supposed that the trial of Othello was connected in some way with a statute of Henry VIII, because the words 'conjuration' and 'witchcraft' occur both in the statute and in the Moor's speech. But these words had been in common use from Chaucer's time in connexion with sorcery.

'MEASURE FOR MEASURE'

The plot of *Measure for Measure* turns largely upon the binding effect of a 'precontract' of marriage. The absence of a ceremony was regarded by the marriage law as an offence, but it did not render such a precontract invalid. The poet has been supposed by some critics to have shown a surprising knowledge of the law on this subject. But he might

SOME EXAGGERATIONS

have gained it by reading the trial of Queen Katherine of Aragon, or from his own personal experience. On the occasion of Shakespeare's marriage to Anne Hathaway a bond was executed by two of his fellow townsmen to indemnify the ecclesiastical authorities against all liability in the event of any lawful impediment to the marriage being afterwards discovered. He could hardly have remained ignorant of the significance of a 'precontract'.

The truth seems to be that Shakespeare displayed a surprising facility in picking up scraps of legal lore and turning them to dramatic account. But there is no necessity for inferring that he must have had any training or practice in the profession of the Law.

BAD LAW IN SHAKESPEARE

Some critics have gone to the opposite extreme, and have dwelt upon what they call 'the bad law' in the plays of Shakespeare. He, like other dramatists, probably cared very little whether this law was strictly accurate, so long as it helped the plot or the dialogue. Sir George Greenwood, with whom the present writer does not always agree, has disposed of this subject in a recent book.[1] For example,

[1] *Shakespeare's Law.* Cecil Palmer, London.

he cites a passage in *Love's Labour's Lost* (i. 1) where three Courtiers are sworn by the King of Navarre to keep certain 'statutes'. A critic has objected to this passage on the ground that Acts of Parliament do not require oaths to render them binding. But the Courtiers are referred to by the King as 'fellow-scholars', and the 'statutes' are not supposed to be Acts of Parliament, but statutes of a College which scholars can correctly be sworn to observe. Again, the Casket Scene in the *Merchant of Venice* has been said to violate the rules of English Law against restraint of marriage, and the reference to Wardship in *All's Well That Ends Well* has been said to overlook the rule of English Law that the lord could not disparage his Ward by a *mésalliance*. But why should a dramatist's law, where the scene is laid in France or Venice or Navarre, be supposed to be strictly conformable to the Laws of England? It is true that Shakespeare sometimes transplanted English Law and customs to foreign countries; but he did not always or necessarily do so.

OTHER EXAGGERATIONS OF SHAKESPEARE'S LEGAL ACQUIREMENTS

CHAPTER XV

OTHER EXAGGERATIONS OF SHAKESPEARE'S LEGAL ACQUIREMENTS

LORD CAMPBELL'S *brochure* made a stir because of his judicial eminence; but the idea that Shakespeare might have been a lawyer's clerk found very few supporters. Indeed, nothing more might have been heard of Shakespeare's supposed connexion with the legal profession, if it had not suited a certain school of theorists to contend that the author of the Shakespearian plays must have been a trained lawyer. They claimed that the notion that he had been a mere attorney's clerk had been 'blown to pieces'. Nevertheless, they utilized Lord Campbell's materials for the purpose of proving that the poet must have been a highly equipped jurist. *Ab hoc ovo* a controversy was hatched, which flew to the United States, where Senator C. K. Davis on one side, and Mr. W. C. Devecmon of the Maryland Bar on the other, became protagonists in debate. The legal allusions which Lord Campbell had discovered numbered less than a hundred. Subsequent writers enlarged them to three hundred. This was accomplished, as Mr. Devecmon pointed out, partly by straining after imaginary legalisms, and partly by counting every single allusion, many of which occurred more than once, and some four or five times.

SOME MORE SUPPOSED LEGALISMS

The following are examples of the legal allusions which some of Lord Campbell's successors detected in the plays. In *Romeo and Juliet* (iii. 1) Escalus threatens to '*amerce*' the brawlers of Verona with '*a fine*'. In the same play the apothecary objects to selling a poison because death is the punishment for him who '*utters*' it. In *Antony and Cleopatra* (v. 2) Cæsar's messenger assures Cleopatra that his master is a 'conqueror, that will *pray in aid* for kindness, where he for grace is kneel'd to'. Again, we are told that, in half a dozen places, Shakespeare used the word '*cheater*', either in its original sense of an escheator or officer who enforced escheats or forfeitures to the Crown,

OTHER EXAGGERATIONS

or in its derivative sense of a 'swindler' or 'cheat'. Frequently the poet uses the word 'exception' in the sense of an 'objection', and once he uses 'proviso' in the sense of a 'condition'. All these expressions were in literary use in or before Shakespeare's time, as appears from the standard dictionaries.

Again, we are told that a reference by Isabella in *Measure for Measure* (ii. 2) to God as the 'top of judgment' is tinged by the poet's legal studies, although the same figure had been used by Sophocles and by Dante. Elsewhere it is said that to mention 'overseers' of a will was characteristic of a law-clerk's experiences, although there was a well-known proverb in the poet's day that 'two executors and one overseer make three thieves', and it was quite common for testators to appoint overseers to supervise or assist the executors of a will. Then we meet with the far-fetched suggestion that, when Falstaff complained to his landlady of having been robbed, and asked, 'Shall I not take mine ease in mine inn?' (1 *Henry IV*, iii. 3) he was claiming the benefit of a rule of law that a lodger's goods were not distrainable for rent due by the lodging-house keeper! Then we have a quaint criticism from a learned K.C. of Shakespeare's application of the Criminal Law. Noticing that Othello was accused of 'stealing Desdemona's heart by spells', this critic seriously observed that the Moor should have been indicted for the 'abduction' of the girl. The writer was testing the plot of a Venetian romance by the technical standards of the Old Bailey. It is right to say that this suggestion is less unreasonable than some others which it would be tedious to enumerate.

NON-TECHNICAL LEGALISMS

Some fifty words or phrases, which were really quite non-technical, have been gleaned from the plays, and have been quoted to prove that Shakespeare must have been a lawyer—for example, 'guilty', 'acquit', 'warrant', 'witness', 'render', 'determine', 'toll'. Such words as these are not monopolies of the legal profession. These and many similar expressions are used freely both by poets and by prose writers. Some of them represent the quota which the science of the Law has contributed to the small change of language's currency. Others, although they have a well recognized legal meaning, belong to the storehouse of general literature. For instance, 'colour' is used by Shakespeare in such senses as 'pretence', 'specious reason', or 'cloak'. The word also has a legal meaning,

OTHER EXAGGERATIONS

and has been claimed as one of Shakespeare's legalisms, although the poet hardly uses it in a strictly legal sense. Similarly, 'capable' in the sense of capable of inheriting, and 'comforting' in the sense of supporting or being accessory to a traitor or usurper, have been claimed as legalisms of Shakespeare's, although they were in general use in those senses in or before the poet's day.

SHAKESPEARE'S SUPPOSED JURISTIC VANITY

Some followers of Lord Campbell have gone so far as to suggest that Shakespeare took pride in displaying his knowledge of law. But it seems unreasonable to suppose that such a consummate dramatist could have allowed himself to be inspired by such vain pedantry. Dramatists, as a rule, are fully alive to the expediency of interesting and amusing their public, and are not so foolish as to indulge in metaphors or jests which their audiences cannot interpret or understand. The prevalence of legal allusions in Elizabethan dramas affords evidence of the legal knowledge of the playgoers as much as of the playwrights.

SHAKESPEARE AND THE LAW

SIR SIDNEY LEE AND SIR ARTHUR UNDERHILL

Considerable weight is due to the lay opinion of Sir Sidney Lee, who is considered by many students of the Shakespearian writings to have been the most careful and painstaking of the poet's biographers, and to the legal opinion of Sir Arthur Underhill, K.C., who has no superior at the English Bar where the Law of Real Property and Conveyancing is concerned. These two writers are agreed in holding that Shakespeare's legal acquirements were greatly exaggerated by Lord Campbell and by his successors in debate, and in pointing out that many of the allusions which seemed so recondite to them were fresh when Shakespeare made them. They attribute his superior grace and ease in making use of legal topics to his peculiar power of pressing into his service the thoughts and terminology of every science and of every art.

SHAKESPEARE'S REAL RELATION TO THE LAW

After all, is there any mystery about Shakespeare's relation to the Law? He lived in a litigious age, was brought up in a litigious

OTHER EXAGGERATIONS

atmosphere, dabbled personally in the buying of land, and became interested or involved in suits or disputes about such matters as mortgages and commons. He had at his elbow a library containing chronicles which were stored with points of Crown, criminal and constitutional law. He had many opportunities of mingling with lawyers, of hearing about the notable trials of his time, and of learning something about the traditions and the customs of the Inns of Court and Chancery. He had to cater for audiences which were largely composed of lawyers. All the dramatists of that age cultivated the art of picking up scraps of legal lore and turning them to dramatic account. Where his legal allusions surpassed those of his contemporaries was in their quality and their aptness rather than in their quantity or their technicality. It is questionable whether they are more surprising than many other facets of his brilliant mind.

INDEX

ABSQUE HOC, 134
Achilles, 105
Acquit, 92, 156
Ædificium solo cedit, 122
Affeeror, 84
Aguecheek, Sir Andrew, 18, 61
Alibi, 134
All's Well That Ends Well, 76, 112, 126, 136, 150
Antipholus, 74, 114
Antony and Cleopatra, 71, 107, 126, 154
Appellant, 82, 94
Arbitrator, 81
Arraignment, 92
Arrest, 91, 92
Arrest on mesne process, 85
As You Like It, 30, 113, 127, 132, 135
Attorney, 83
Attorney-General, 83

BACON, FRANCIS, xiv–xxxv, 33–34
Bacon, Miss Delia, xix

'Bad law' in Shakespeare, 149, 150
Bailiff, 84
Banquo's ghost, xiv
Bar, The comradeship of the, 84
Bargain and Sale, 112
Barnebe Barnes, 13, 14
Bassanio, 29, 87
Beaston, xxviii
Beatrice, 94
Beaumont, Francis, 17
Belch, Sir Toby, 18, 61–63
Benedick, 29, 94
Benefit of clergy, 96
Benvolio, 102
Birkenhead, The Earl of, 69, 70
Biron, 136
Blanche, 101
Booth, William Stone, xxiii
Browne, Judge, 52, 53
Buckingham, 105
Burbage, Richard, 19
Burghley, Lord, 26, 33, 62
Burning to death, 101

INDEX

CADE, JACK, 18, 93, 96, 116
Cæsar, Julius, *vide* Julius Cæsar
Camden, William, 32
Campbell, Lord, xxix, xxx, 95, 125, 141–148, 153–4
Capable, 157
Catlyne, Sir Robert, 48
Certiorari, 11
Cesario, 61
Challenge, 92
Chancellor, Lord, 70, 106
Chapman, George, 122
Cheater, 84
Chronicles, The, 9, 105, 144–145
Chudleigh's Case, 75, 77
Clement's Inn, 37–43
Cobham, Lord, 60
Coke, Sir Edward, 59–62, 70, 71, 75
Collier, Mr. Payne, 142
Colour, 156
Comedy of Errors, 17, 25–27, 64–66, 114
Comforting, 157
Commons, 111, 114–118
Connecticut, xxi
Connes, Professor, 34
Constable, 84
Constitutional Law, 105, 106
Convict, 92
Corbet's Case, 76
Cordelia, 132
Costard, 136
Counsellor, 83
Counterpart, 137
Court Crier, 84
Cover, 135
Crab, 102
Craven, 95
Criminal Law, 91–103
Crown Law, 91
Cum privilegio ad imprimendum, 134

DAVIES, ARCHDEACON, 42
Davis, Senator C. K., 153
Defendant, 82
Dekker, Thomas, 10
'De La Grange, Prince,' 26
Demblan, M., 33
Derby, Ferdinando Stanley, 5th Earl of, 28
Derby, William Stanley, 6th Earl of, 33–34
Desdemona, 93, 105, 132, 156
Determine, 156
Dethicke, Sir William, 32
Devecmon, Mr. W. C., 154
Dick the Butcher, 96
Dogberry, 93, 136
Dormiunt aliquando leges, moriuntur nunquam, 121
Drayton, Michael, 8
Dromio, 74, 86
Dumain, Captain, 112
Dying declarations, 126

INDEX

EDGAR, 147
Edward I, 18
Edward IV, 105, 106
Elizabeth, Queen, xv, xxxi, 26–30, 38, 49, 70
Enclosure, *see* Inclosure
Enfeoff, 112
Entail, 72–77
Epicene, The, 10
Escalus, 81, 154
Escheater, 84
Essex, The Earl of, 29, 32, 50
Estates Tail, 72–76
Eure, William, 62, 63
Every Man in His Humour, 18
Exaggeration of Shakespeare's Legal Acquirements, 141–159
Executioner, 103

FALSTAFF, SIR JOHN, xxi, 37–41, 85, 103, 104, 112, 122, 155
Faulconbridge, 144
Fee-farm, 112
Fee-simple, 111, 112
Fine and imprisonment, 103
Fines and recoveries, 72–76
Fitton, Mary, 31
Fittons, The, 31
Flesh, man and wife is one, 125
Florizel, 29
Ford, John, 17
Fortescue, Sir John, 19, 22
Franklin, Benjamin, xxviii

GARDENER, SAMUEL, 60
Gascoigne, George, 18
Gascoigne, Sir William, 47, 49, 81, 103, 106
Gaunt, John of, 38–41
Glendower, 144
Gloucester, The Duke of, 95
Gollancz, Sir Israel, *see Dedication*
Grand Jury, 82
Gratiano, 29, 87
Gray's Inn, xv, xxxvii, 18, 25–34, 47, 55, 66
Greene, Thomas, 19
Greenwood, Sir George, 149
Guilty, 156

HABEAS CORPUS, 11
Hal, Prince, 20, 48, 49
Hales, Sir James, 51–54
Hales *v*. Petit, 51–54
Hamlet, xiii, xv, xxxiii, 11, 51–54, 92, 104, 111, 112, 125, 134, 143
Hanged, drawn and quartered, 101
Hangman, 103
Helena, 136
Henry IV, Part I, 112
Henry IV, Part II, 20, 25, 40, 41, 48, 49, 103, 104
Henry V, 49, 106, 132
Henry VI, Part II, 81, 95, 96, 101, 102, 112, 132

INDEX

Henry VI, Part III, 104
Henry VIII, 106, 127, 145
Hereford, Duke of, 95
Heresy, 101
Hoby, Sir Posthumus, 62, 63
Hortensio, 102
Hotspur, 144
Hulme, Sir Henry, 27
Hunsdon, Lord, 28

IAGO, 87, 105
Impressment, 103, 104, 105
Imprimis, 134
Inclosure, 115, 118
Indenture, 131
Indictment, 133
Inner Temple, 17, 19, 37, 38, 42, 64
Inns of Chancery, 37–43
Inns of Court, 17–34
Interlocutory Proceedings, 85–87, 125, 126
Interrogatories, 86, 87

JAMES I, 17, 49
Jaquenetta, 137
Jaques, 132, 133
Jargon, Legal, 131–137
Johnson, Doctor Samuel, xxv
Jonson, Ben, 10, 12, 18, 26, 29, 134, 145
Judge, 81
Julius Cæsar, 71, 107, 114
Jury, 82

KATHARINA AND PETRUCHIO, 95, 96, 102
Katherine, Queen, 92, 146, 149
King John, 125, 126
King Lear, 30, 85, 102, 132, 147
King's Attorney, 83
Kyd, Thomas, 143

LAERTES, 26
Lambert, John, 19
Launce, 102
Law of Property Act, 69
Lawful Prize, 105
Lease, 113, 114
Le Beau, 135
Lee, Sir Sidney, 37, 43, 158
Lefranc, Professor, 33
Leicester, The Earl of, 64
Lincoln's Inn, 25, 26, 33, 42
Lodge, Thomas, 18
Love's Labour's Lost, 30, 117–118, 134, 136, 150
Lucio, 94
Lucrece, The Rape of, 29, 84, 91, 92
Lucy, Sir Thomas, 37–43

MACBETH, 113, 124
Mainor, 136
Malone, Edmund, xxix, 142
Malvolio, 62, 63
Manningham, John, 19
Manwood, Sir Roger, 63–66

INDEX

Mary Portington's Case, 73
Mary Queen of Scots, 50
Maxims, Legal, 121–127
Measure for Measure, 82, 94, 121, 131, 148
Merchant of Venice, 86, 146, 147, 150
Merry Wives of Windsor, 38–40, 74, 84, 112, 122
Merton, Statute of, 115
Middle Temple, 17, 18, 19, 60, 61, 62
Midsummer Night's Dream, 30
Mississippi, xviii, xx, xxvi, xxvii
Missouri, xxv, xxvii
Mistress Overdone, 85
Moots, 22
Mortgage, 9, 111, 112, 113
Mortimers, The, 21, 144
Mountjoy *v.* Bellot, 86
Much Ado About Nothing, 82, 94, 136

NASHE, THOMAS, 11, 12, 143
Nerissa, 86
Nevada, xxvii
Nonsuit, 87
Non-technical Legalisms, 156
Norfolk, Dukes of, 50, 95, 106
Noverint Universi, 135

OATHS, 82, 126
Octavius, 114

Officers of Justice, 84
Old Bailey, 92
Olivia, 62, 63
Omittance no Quittance, 127
Ordeal of Battle, 94
Othello, 87, 93, 105, 132, 148
Oxford, 17th Earl of, 26, 33, 34

PAINE, ALBERT BIGELOW, xxii, xxiii
Pandarus, 94, 112
Paritor, 84
Parolles, 112
Peace Officer, 84
Peale, George, 11, 12
Peine Forte et Dure, 12, 93–94
Pembroke, William Herbert, 3rd Earl of, xxvii, 31, 33, 34
Penzance, Lord, xxx
Perpetuities, 75–77
Pheasant and Advocate, 54, 55
Phesant, Peter, 54, 55
Philip the Bastard, 101
Plaintiff, 82
Plantagenet, Richard, 21
Plautus, 66
Pleas, 92
Polonius, 26
Pompey, 107
Portia, 86
Possession, 125
Præmunire, 13, 115
Pray in aid, 154

[165]

INDEX

Precontract of Marriage, 148, 149
Prerogative Law, 103
Presents, By These, 135
Procedendo, 11
Procedure, 7, 8
Process-server, 84
Proteus, 107
Punishments, 101, 102
Puns, 74, 117, 135–137
Purchased, 69–71
Purpoole, Prince of, 27
Purveyance, 104

RALEIGH, SIR WALTER, 50, 60–62
Real Property, The Law of, 7, 69–77, 111–118
Recoveries, 72–76
Remainder, 75, 77
Render, 156
Richard II, 94, 124
Richard III, 83, 105, 106, 133
Robertson, J. M., 10
Rogers, Henry H., xvii
Romeo and Juliet, xxiv, 29, 102, 112, 135, 146, 154
Rosalind, 135
Rowe, Nicolas, 42
Rushton, W. L., 123–126
Rutland, Roger Manners, 5th Earl of, 26, 29, 31, 32

SAY, LORD, 81, 96
Scriveners, 84

Seals, 131
Se offendendo, 134
Sergeant, 83
Several, 116–118
Shallow, Justice, 37–41
Shelley, Percy Bysshe, 31
Shelley's Case, 69–71, 77
Shylock, 147
Sidney, Sir Henry, 30
Sidney, Sir Philip, 30–31
Slender, 39
Solicitor, 83
Somerset, The Earl of, 22
Sonnets, The, 13, 14, 112, 113, 117
Southampton, Henry Wriothesley, 3rd Earl of, xxxvii, 26, 28, 30, 32, 107
Speed, 115
Spenser, Edmund, 12, 14, 30
Star Chamber, 39, 50, 62, 63
Steal, 136
Strange, Lord, *see* Derby, 5th Earl of
Stratford-on-Avon, xxvii, xxviii, xxxvi, 9, 34, 37, 42, 111, 116, 118
'Sue his Livery,' 145
Suffolk, Duke of, 106
Suffolk, Earl of, 22
Supersedeas, 13
Supremacy of the Crown, 145
Suum cuique, 134
Sylvia, 107

INDEX

TAGS, LEGAL, 133–134
Taltarum's Case, 73
Taming of the Shrew, 84, 95, 102
Tempest, The, 30
Temple, The, 17–22
Thersites, 105
Toll, 156
Torture, 102, 103
Tower of London, 21, 30
Towse, 19
Tripartite, 144
Troilus and Cressida, xxiv, 94, 105, 107, 112, 124
Twain, Mark, xvi–xxix, xxxi, xxxvii
Twelfth Night, 17, 59, 62
Two Gentlemen of Verona, 102, 107, 114

UNDERHILL, SIR ARTHUR, K.C., 75, 158
Underwood v. Manwood, 65, 66
Utter, 154

VALENTINE, 29, 107, 114
Vanity, Shakespeare's supposed juristic, 157
Vassalage, 107, 108
Venus and Adonis, 29, 85, 131
Vernon, 22
Villeinage, 107, 108

WAGER OF BATTLE, 94
Walshe, Sergeant, 52, 53
War of the Roses, 104
Wardship, 150
Wards, the Court of, 26
Warrant, 156
Warwick (The Kingmaker), 21, 104
Winter's Tale, 103
Witchcraft, 101, 148
Witness, 156
Wolsey, Cardinal, 92, 146

ZEPHERIA, 13, 14

www.ingramcontent.com/pod-product-compliance
Lightning Source LLC
Chambersburg PA
CBHW032023230426
43671CB00005B/182